Venice of America
'Coney Island of the Pacific'

To James
Jeffrey Stanton

by Jeffrey Stanton

Donahue Publishing

Design and art work by Jeffrey Stanton.

Printed by Donahue Printing on both 4 color and 2 color Heidelberg Speedmaster presses.

Donahue Publishing
5716 W. Jefferson Blvd.
Los Angeles, Ca. 90016
(213) 938-4545

Acknowledgements

Everyone said that it was a bad time to do historic research considering the number of libraries and major photo collections closed in the Los Angeles area in 1987. If I hadn't written a previous Venice history book nearly ten years earlier and accumulated a large photo library, I would have given up.

The prime source for the text were the microfilm versions of the Venice Vanguard newspaper (1911-1956) available at the Culver City Library, and the Santa Monica Evening Outlook (1903-1968) available at a Santa Monica branch library. The problem with newspapers is that much that was written about the amusement industry is based on exaggerated press releases, and some of it was never built. Fortunately my extensive aerial photo collection throughout the 20's and 30's confirms most of what is written in this book.

There are many people who I would like to thank for helping me with this book. Barbara Williams for her background on carousels; Mike Chew for his knowledge of roller coasters and the lives of Prior and Church; John Payne for his memories of the Venice and Ocean Park Piers from 1938-1951; Fred McGinnis for his recollection of Pacific Ocean Park and Hoppyland; Dan Tompkins who had the publicity contract and photographed Pacific Ocean Park for its owners in 1958; Jo Ann Hilston and Lee Brown for allowing me to photograph their postcard collections; Stan Matthews for editing the manuscript; Tom Moran for reading the manuscript for historical accuracy; Jim Mitchell for helping me with his Amiga computer to photo enhance a carousel photo; and Mark Wanamaker, owner of Bison Archives, who made my copy negatives from borrowed photographs and whose large photo library was of immense help.

Suprisingly the Venice community was of little help with my research. Despite a big article by the Evening Outlook newspaper about my search for rare amusement pier photos, virtually no one responded and those with known large collections made excuses. Regrettably several important photographs of rides like the Niagara Barrel, the Great American Racing Derby, and the Dentzel Carousel on the rebuilt Venice Pier, and Over the Top on the Ocean Park Pier were unobtainable for my book. If any reader has these photos or any others, please write.

I can only sum up this manuscript by saying that Venice must have been the most wonderful place in the world to grow up in during the teens and twenties. I'm sorry I missed it. I only wish we were allowed to rebuild the amusement piers and restore Venice to what it was during its peak of popularity.

Photo Credits

U.C.L.A. (1, 104 right); Los Angeles Library (4 bottom, 18, 30, 73, 128, 141 top); Title Insurance (4 top, 8 top, 14, 17, 26, 80); Kurt Simon (5, 7); Santa Monica Library (10 top, 155); Bruce Henstell (11, 36, 86, 127, 131); Los Angeles County Museum of History Seaver Center (20, 21 top, 22, 25, 26, 87, 90, 103); Bison Archives (21 bottom, 39 top, 54, 75 bottom, 76, 78, 81, 85, 88, 93, 98, 99 bottom, 100, 102, 106, 112, 123, 133, 137, 141, 143); George Sheady (23, 124); V. R. Plukas (24, 40, 41, 59 bottom, 61, 79, 104 bottom, 104 bottom, 105, 122, 132 all, 134, 136); Joanne Hilston (27, 32, 37, 53, 70, 75 top); Henry E. Huntington Library (29, 34, 35, 38, 39 bottom, 44, 58, 60, 62, 66, 67, 71, 82, 135); Ken Jewett (33 bottom, 118, 120, 129 all, 139, 146); Barbara Williams (42 top, 46 top left, 46 bottom rt, 51 all, 52, 64 top, 68 right, 101); Fred McGinnis (48 top, 115, 158 top, 167 top); Dr. Bubar (56); Carousel Art Magazine (63 top); Santa Monica Historical Society (63 bottom); Ken Strickfaden (84, 92 bottom, 108, 111, 114, 119, 121); Henry Vignolle (92 top); Fred Basten (96); Roger Torpin (104 top, 144); Tony Bill (116); Los Angeles Times (124); Tim Sullivan (125); John Payne (145 all); Dan Tompkins (147, 150, 151, 152, 153, 154, 156 all, 158 bottom, 159, 160 all, 161, 162, 163, 164 all, 165, 166 all, 167 bottom, 169 left); Security Pacific (157); Bill Reagh (168); Darnell Gadberry (176 bottom). All remaining photographs and postcards were purchased by the author from various antique and postcard dealers. Photographs in the last chapter were taken by the author and most are available along with many others in postcard form from the author's Venice Postcard Company.

CONTENTS

CHAPTER 1

Building Venice of America (1904-1906)

It was the beginning of the 20th century, a time when anything seemed possible and men like Abbot Kinney, a wealthy cigarette manufacturer, had their dreams. It was an exciting time in Southern California, a time of opportunity when Easterners and Midwesterners, who were lured to the area by the publicity of inexpensive land and a mild winter climate, emigrated by the thousands to the Los Angeles basin.

Men like Kinney, railroad tycoon Huntington and others subdivided the original Spanish land grants to provide town sites for the thousands of emigrants who needed places to live and play. Yet of all the plans and promotions of inland town sites and beachfront

Abbot Kinney (1850-1920), founder of Venice.

The Abbot Kinney Pier at Windward Avenue had a 2400 seat Auditorium and a Ship Cafe built on pilings.

Grand opening celebration, July 4, 1905, on Windward Avenue. (righ

St. Marks Square at Windward and Ocean Front Walk. Bandstand is on right, St Marks Hotel on left.

communities, one captured the imagination and fancy of the public — Abbot Kinney's Venice of America.

Abbot Kinney had been feuding with his three Ocean Park Improvement Company partners for some time when they met in the company office in January 1904 to divide their beachfront property. Kinney and his former partner Francis Ryan had purchased the tract of land just south of Santa Monica in 1895. Here they had developed a modest seaside resort by building a golf course, tennis courts, country clubhouse, boardwalk and a fishing pier at the foot of Pier Avenue. They gave the Santa Fe Railroad a small tract of land with the understanding that they would build a pavilion there, and a much larger tract to the Y.M.C.A. in hopes that the construction of an auditorium and bathhouse would attract conventions and assemblies to Ocean Park. The remainder of the property was subdivided into small 25 x 100 foot, $45 lots which sold well considering the economic slump of the 1890's. Unsold lots were rented for $15 per year with the understanding that 'neat and substantial cottages' would be built upon them. Transportation to the resort was arranged when a spur of the new Los Angeles electric railroad was extended south from Santa Monica to Hill Street in 1896.

When Ryan died in 1899, his widow remarried. Thomas H. Dudley proved to be a satisfactory business partner for Kinney, as they began to pursue active development plans. However, in 1902, Dudley sold his half of the company to Alexander R. Fraser, George Merritt Jones and Henry R. Gage, three businessmen who didn't see eye to eye with their strong-willed and imaginative partner. After nearly two years of constant feuding, Kinney and his partners decided to divide their holdings with the flip of a coin.

One wintery afternoon the four partners gathered at the company's office. One of the partners tossed a coin high into the air. Kinney called "Tails" and the coin landed on the floor tails up. The three partners contemplated what they would do with their mostly worthless water-logged land.

The southern half of their Ocean Park property consisted mostly of sand dunes fronting unusable swampy marsh, while the northern half of had become a very popular and fashionable resort. A large number of beach cottages had been built and some permanent residents were beginning to settle in the area. A casino, containing a restaurant and vaudeville theater, was built beside the pier in summer 1903 as a replacement for the Auditorium that burned in 1897. There were plans for an immense bathing pavilion complete with plunge,

The promenade on Ocean Front Walk extended north to the Fraser Pier in Ocean Park; 1906.

The Ocean Park Bathhouse, built in 1905, contained a hot salt-water plunge. (above)

Ingersoll's Toboggan Railroad built in 1903 adjacent to the Ocean Park Pier was a forerunner of the roller coaster. (below)

ballroom and amphitheater to be built on the boardwalk south of the pier.

Kinney examined the coin carefully in his hand. He looked north to the beautiful shore line of Ocean Park, and south to the miserable undeveloped salt marshes. It was a decision that he had previously thought about long and hard.

"I'll take the salt marshes", he replied.

His partners gasped in amazement, smiled knowingly as if to say "There, didn't I tell you he was crazy", shook hands and the deal was closed. "You'd agotten the marsh if we'd won." his ex-partners jibbed.

Kinney retorted, "not if you see what I see."

Abbot Kinney was a dreamer who saw vast potential in that seemingly worthless salt marsh acreage. He knew that it would have to be canaled and drained for any development to take place. Some of his earliest known plans show his intent to make a 15 acre island in Venice complete with hotels, cafes, theaters and all kinds of the amusements that made Coney Island famous. He planned to charge ten cents admission to the island and extra for the attractions. Kinney also had additional property adjacent to the island if he needed to expand.

Although he had been kicking this idea around in his head for years and was most likely the reason for the rift between his partners, Kinney began formulating much more grandiose plans. As a world-travelled connoisseur of art and scenic beauty, he recognized the similarity between his marshy land and that of Venice, Italy. As a broadly educated romanticist he envisioned a beach community that would foster a cultural Renaissance, an American Renaissance that would begin on the shores of the Pacific.

Fortunately, he had the money to carry out his plans. He had amassed a fortune through the manufacturing of Sweet Caporal cigarettes prior to moving from Washington D.C. area to Los Angeles in 1880.

Abbot Kinney commissioned architects Norman Marsh and C.H. Russell to prepare a town plan. He also hired F.V. Dunham to travel east and visit various seaside resorts like Sandy Hook, N.J., Coney Island, N.Y. and Atlantic City, N.J.

It is obvious that the Venice plan owed much to the Chicago World's Columbian Exposition which had been built on reclaimed lowlands along the Lake Michigan shoreline in 1893. The fair featured a central basin, a meandering lagoon and gondoliers who plied the canal network. A replica of a ship was 'moored' alongside a pier and a railroad shuttled fairgoers around the site. A wide pedestrian thoroughfare called the

Midway Plaisance was built adjacent to the main exhibit area. It was flanked on both sides by food vendors, entertainment and curiosities from foreign lands, games of skill and chance and thrill rides that included the first giant Ferris wheel.

Although the Venice plan was much more modest in scale, Kinney and his architects followed the Chicago World's Fair example in creating a detailed comprehensive town layout. Like the planned communities of later generations, Venice would separate housing areas from commercial and entertainment areas.

During the era of mass transit, locating any new development near transportation facilities was an important consideration. Venice owed its initial physical shape as much to the railroad tracks that surrounded it as to the high and low points that determined the canal network. The Los Angeles Pacific had first extended tracks south from Santa Monica in 1901. A short line was completed in 1902 directly from Los Angeles. Its route was across bean fields, following what is now Venice Boulevard, then north along Electric Way to Ocean Park. By 1903 Kinney had persuaded E. H. Harriman to extend its tracks directly to the beachfront.

Canal dredging began on August 15, 1904. This first contract was let for excavation of the Grand Canal, a half mile long, seventy foot wide, four foot deep channel. An army of men, teams of horses and several steam shovels removed tons of dirt and sand, using it to build up other low lying areas, until a network of canals was completed. Additional sand mixed in a slurry with salt water was sluiced through large pipes from the sand dunes just beyond the beach. Cost was no object, as workers were paid eight dollars a day - a handsome wage in those times.

Although the canal area was less than one square mile, the architects, by departing from the familiar grid pattern, created the illusion that the canal area was quite extensive. Initially two linear miles of canals were dug, mostly forty feet wide and curbed with concrete. The entire fan shaped network was connected to the ocean by two large pipes which ran under Windward Avenue, and was flushed twice daily by tidal action.

A second set of canals, which connected to Kinney's network, was soon dug south of his Venice of America tract by Strong and Dickerson. These canals in the Venice Canal Subdivision, which were dug a year later, extended south to the entrance of Ballona Lagoon. They helped circulate and flush Kinney's canals after the two pipes proved to be barely adequate.

Work on the entire Venice of America development

The Ocean Park Bathhouse looked like an ornate Arabian palace.

Visitors relax at the beach just south of the Ocean Park Pier. The Toboggan Railroad is in the background.

Pier Street in Ocean Park at the entrance to the Ocean Park Pier; 1905.

Bandstand and Casino at the Ocean Park Pier; 1905.

Venice's lagoon area was the site of numerous aquatic events; 1906.

Windward Avenue was lined with hotels, shops, and restaurants; 1905.

Arrival of Los Angeles Pacific's interurban electric cars at the corner of Windward and Trolley Way (Pacific Avenue).

progressed rapidly. By September work had begun on the 1700 foot long, 30 foot wide pier, and the foundations for the electric power plant were progressing. A country club house just north of the tract was being built for golf, tennis and croquet. That November the public, convinced at last that Kinney was more than a foolish dreamer, rushed to purchase lots in a flurry of excitement.

The Venice of America tract wasn't exactly inexpensive. The 592 residential lots, of which 400 faced the water, included public utilities. Depending on location they sold for as much as $2700. This was a considerable sum relative to the price of other seaside resort developments at the time. Nonetheless, November sales reached $386,000.

By January 1905 contracts for over $300,000 worth of buildings had been awarded. The building of the palatial St Marks and other hotels on Windward were proceeding smoothly, while out on the pier the Ship Hotel and the Auditorium were taking shape. Kinney announced that the Summer Assembly, a Chautauqua like event representing the best in modern thought and art, would be held in the auditorium structure.

Kinney's architects incorporated some rather innovative building concepts into the town. By digging several interconnecting tunnels under the alleyways in the Windward business district, they were able to pump hot salt water to the hotel rooms, and rid the area of unsightly power lines. At the same time they had easy access for repairs. Other tunnels, leading from hotel basements, allowed guests to cross under Ocean Front Walk to the beach in bathing attire. This was convenient because in those puritanical times bathing attire was banned on the boardwalk. They were also able to reduce initial costs by creating walk streets in part of the development. By substituting sidewalks for paved streets in the noncanaled residential district adjacent to the beach, they achieved a courtyard effect for these small lots and safety for the children.

Disaster struck in February and March. The heaviest storms in more than a generation wrecked the pier and severely damaged the Auditorium and other structures on it. Even the Pavilion on the pier's inland end collapsed when the outer end of pilings washed away. The entire construction site was flooded and damages were in excess of $50,000. The beach was littered with one vast pile of driftwood from both Kinney's and Ocean Park's piers. Critics called his project "Kinney's Folly".

Although Abbot Kinney was undaunted, it became clear to him that the pier would have to be protected.

He secured the government's permission to erect a 500 foot semi-circular breakwater of Riverside granite. It cost him $100,000 and required rail shipment of 70,000 tons of quarried stone in nearly 1000 railroad cars.

Rebuilding the pier and damaged buildings was of the highest priority as summer was approaching rapidly. The auditorium with a capacity of 3600 was constructed in a record twenty eight days of overtime work and was ready for the opening of the Assembly on July 2nd. The Ship Hotel, a 182 foot long replica of Juan Cabrillo's galleon built on pilings beside the pier, was repaired and ready to accomodate 1000 dinner guests. And the three story Spanish styled Venice Bathhouse built adjacent to the lagoon at a cost of $40,000 contained a 70 by 70 foot salt water plunge, two dozen private baths and 520 changing rooms.

On June 30th Abbot Kinney opened the flood gates to two thirty-inch diameter pipes that extended hundreds of feet into the Pacific beneath the pier. Salt water, pouring in at the rate of 500 gallons a second during high tide, soon filled the lagoon and surrounding canal network. Two evenings later Kinney tripped the circuits to the 17,000 electric lamps that lined the streets, piers and canals. The effect was magical.

Independence Day 1905 was a day of celebration. Forty thousand people poured into Venice of America, most coming by interurban railroad or "green cars" as they were called in those days. Banners strung across Windward Avenue fluttered overhead, while Arend's forty piece Italian band played on the bandstand at the foot of the pier.

Visitors marveled at the two block long, column-lined arcaded street that connected the beach to the lagoon. By mandate structures were embellished in a pseudo-Italian style, at least their facades. With upper floors extending over the arcades, shaded walkways provided relief from the noon day sun.

Hotels like the St. Marks, Venice and Gondolier, which lined the north side of the street, featured hot salt water piped to each room to be used for therapeutic value. Downstairs on the arcade level were restaurant, tobacco merchants, drug and sundries stores and souvenir vendors.

Entertainment ranged from high cultural to popular sporting events. The Assembly meeting in the pier auditorium offered lectures and speeches, alternating with patriotic songs sung by the Venice Children's Chorus. Benjamin Fay Mills, a popular evangelist, delivered the opening remarks. Thousands of other visitors watched the 2nd Annual California swimming and diving contest

Windward Avenue's colonnaded walkways gave shelter from the hot sun.

Visitors listened to Arend's Band at the pier bandstand.

at the lagoon from the large tiered amphitheater. For those who just wanted to relax, there was the choice of the beach or a chauffeured gondola ride through the canals by one of 24 imported Italian gondoliers. At dusk a grand fireworks display reflected in the lagoon's water capped the opening day festivities.

Kinney certainly offered the public a potpourri for all tastes. His initial aim was to attract people, show them a good time and then get them to buy lots. His plan definitely worked, for realtors sold most of the remaining lots during the three day opening celebration.

Ocean Park had a small celebration of its own that Fourth of July. Kinney's ex-partners dedicated their new bathing pavilion. The $150,000 building, with its graceful dome and turrets, was the pride of Ocean Park. Its interior contained a 70 by 70 foot salt water plunge and hundreds of dressing rooms. Patrons could rent the latest in bathing attire. At night when the electric lights were ablaze, its thickly beaded towers made it look like a fairy palace silhouetted against the sky.

It was apparent that these men weren't going to let Ocean Park become a second class resort. Plans were advanced to built a semi-circular Horseshoe Pier that would incorporate the two smaller recently built piers at Pier and Marine Avenues. A large 250 x 210 foot auditorium with music hall and balconied outdoor bandstand would be built on the land end.

The pier area already had a few amusements. These included a small tented carousel and a ferris wheel, which were setup along the boardwalk near the pier to entertain the children during the busy summer seasons. The first permanent ride wasn't built until the 1903 summer season when L.G. Ingersoll built his two-passenger toboggan coaster on pilings part way over the ocean adjacent to the casino. Each two-passenger car was pulled to the top in this gentle forerunner to the roller coaster, and then released to coast down along a wide but gentle oval track containing only a few three foot dips along its length. It even appealed to some of the more adventuresome vacationing adults.

The public, however, was much more interested in Venice and returned often for a day at the beach that summer. But, unfortunately for Kinney, most people, didn't share his enthusiasm for culture. Even though he hired the best lecturers and performers of the time including Helen Hunt Jackson, author of 'Ramona' and the Chicago Symphony Orchestra, the Chautaqua-like Assembly lost $16,000 the first summer. The Assembly failed to attract patrons simply because there were too many distractions to lure them elsewhere. They preferred to play hooky on the beach.

Venice Lagoon and Midway Plaisance alongside the Grand Canal; 1906.

View of the Midway Plaisance and its attractions.

Helter Skelter, a giant slide at Windward and Trolley Way.

Camel riding at the Streets of Cairo exhibit at the Midway Plaisance.

Gondolier on the Grand Canal.

Kinney, who was an astute businessman, discarded the costly Assembly and instead concentrated on the tastes of day-trip and summer holiday guests. By fall, he arranged to have rides and amusements from Portland's Lewis and Clark Exposition shipped south.

Kinney was also disappointed with the lack of accomodations. Most lot buyers had previously agreed to build by opening day, but many had broken contracts and sold to speculators. The Kinney Company, in an attempt to serve the demanding public who attended the Assembly and needed housing, constructed a temporary tent city on the canal banks. It proved to be one of the most popular features of Venice life.

The Midway Plaisance's eleven buildings built along the edge of swimming lagoon opened on a intermittent rainy weekend in mid January 1906. The area was patterned after the amusement thoroughfares of the great 19th and 20th century expositions; its name taken from the 1893 Chicago World's Fair. It featured foreign exhibits, amusements and freak shows from both Port-

land's Lewis and Clark Exposition and the St Louis World's Fair. Although it was the beginning of the honky-tonk carnival atmosphere which would in later years be found on the pier, Kinney and some of the nearby residents were aghast at the some of low class shows that it offered. Still, it was the best congregation of amusement devices on the Pacific Coast, the public loved it and it made a handsome profit.

Barkers with hand-held megaphones stood outside trying to induce visitors into the various shows. A troupe of sword fighters, magicians and Hindu fakirs led by Princess Rajah demonstrated the sports and pastimes of the Orient in the large ornate twin-turreted Oriental Theater. Nearby in the Spanish Theater, decorated in Moorish style with bright red tiles and Alhambra designs, was Chiquita, the smallest and most perfect woman in the world. The 30 year old performer, only 28 inches tall and weighing 32 pounds, danced and sang in three languages. Further up the midway Madame Canihac, queen of the lion tamers and Senor Oroldo,

View of the Midway Plaisance. The tent in the background contained a portable carousel.

The bathhouse on the corner of Windward and Coral Canal was a heated salt-water plunge. (above)

Gondoliers along Alderbaren Canal, now Market Street; 1906. (left)

Italian gondoliers give excursion rides down Lion Canal. Tent city is on the far right along the banks of Grand Canal. (right)

The Venice Bathhouse contained a 70 foot square hot salt water plunge and over 500 dressing rooms.

Entertainment included ten cent camel rides.

The St. Marks and other hotels lined the north side of Windward Avenue.

king of blood thirsty jaguars and leopards, subdued large cats in Akron's Wild Animal Show.

The crowds were enchanted with the foreign exhibits. 'Streets of Cairo' offered a reproduction of Algazera Plaza in Cairo complete with turks, merchants, bazaars and camels. Visitors could seek out a fortune teller, sip small cups of Turkish coffee, see the Egyptian mummy collection and even ride a camel. Over in 'Fair Japan' beyond the entrance gate of Nico was a rendition of the streets of Tokio and a three story tea house. The 'Klondike' exhibit, from the Canadian gold rush featured an Eskimo exhibit and a placer mine complete with stream, cabin and mountain scenery.

Most of the amusements were either quaint walk through shows or early fun houses. The largest clown head ever built with blinking eyes and a laughing face adorned the 'Temple of Mirth' facade. Inside were fun devices like the 'Cave of the Winds', moving platforms, a 'Passage to the Rockies' and over 35 convex and concave mirrors that reflected one's image in all shapes and deformations. Nearby was the 'Maze' with over 150 mirrors that dared a person to find a way out.

'Darkness at Dawn' was one concessionaire's's vision of Hell. The journey began with the torchlit Chamber of Death complete with creepy decaying skeletons and musty wooden coffins. Visitors descended by elevator to the region of Hades where they visited the caves of Dante's inferno. The finale was a visit to the palace of his majesty, the Devil.

Kinney tried his best to attract and please the public that first winter and early spring. As an added attraction he invited the Sells-Floto circus to spend their winter quarters in Venice near the Midway Plaisance. Acts like Buffalo Bill and Zora, Sharpe's equestrian team and the Eddy Family Acrobats entertained tourists in the bigtop on weekends. He hired Ellery's Band to replace Armand's Band at the Venetian Gardens on the pier, and began paying half fare rebates to visitors on roundtrip Los Angeles Pacific electric car rides from downtown Los Angeles.

A miniature railroad with a Prairie 2-6-2 engine was installed in the spring as a municipal transportation system for those who dreaded the thought of rowing a boat to market. Its two mile loop on 18 guage track crossed over graceful bridges that spanned residential district canals with romantic names like Venus, Lion, Altair and Aldebarren. Its main terminal and turnaround point was on Windward at Trolley Way. The public, particularly children, loved the ride and the price was right, a nickel.

Camel ride down Windward Avenue; 1906.

Arched colonnades, Windward Avenue; 1906. (opposite page)

Ocean Park business interests were willing to enter the competition for the tourist's amusement dollar in a more substantial manner. As soon as Kinney announced the opening of the Midway Plaisance the previous fall they talked of building a Coney Island style amusement area, but only if they could convince promoters to build a scenic railroad, haunted castle, chutes and grottos on the pier or nearby on the sand.

The area south of the pier was ruled out since all of the beach from Navy to Horizon streets was deeded to the public during the first official meeting of the newly incorporated city in February 1904 for non-commercial use only. They could either build on their nearly completed Horseshoe Pier or on the south side of the pier in Santa Monica. Promoters, watching Kinney closely, took a wait and see attitude in Ocean Park. The only entertainment feature to open that spring was a roller skating rink that occupied a portion of the newly completed Auditorium building.

Venice of America, however, was in the midst of a building boom. The canaled residential area was beginning to take on a more settled look as more beach cottages were built. The maturing eucalyptus and palm trees gave the area a parklike appearance. A roller skating rink opened at Trolleyway near Windward in early May, and Kinney was adding a Japanese exhibit and temple to the Pavilion as well as constructing an enormous Dance Hall on the pier.

While cultural events were relegated to the back burner, Venice scored an unexpected coup when Sarah Bernhardt, the controversial French actress, decided to visit. A syndicate of theater owners had shut her out of the major concert halls on her "Farewell America Tour". When the Los Angeles theaters boycotted her, Abbot Kinney made arrangements for her to use the Venice Auditorium for the two day event May 18th and 19th, 1906.

The red-haired actress arrived in her private railroad car on Friday afternoon. It was promptly switched onto track running out to the Venice Pier, and parked with the observation end facing the ocean and setting sun. That evening she played the staring role in Sardou's 'La Sorciere' before a sold out audience that included many of Southern California's prominent citizens.

The following afternoon she played the lead in 'La Dame aux Camelias', and in the evening Puccini's 'La Tosca'. While few in the audience understood either the French or Italian dialogue, they were appreciative and called her back for twenty curtain calls. Afterwards Kinney and a few of the Midway's entertainers dined

Windward Avenue colonades.

The Auditorium on the Abbot Kinney Pier was used to hold the Chautauqua-like Assembly.

Japanese Pavilion on the Abbot Kinney Pier; 1906.

The miniature railroad took passengers for excursions around the canal area. (left)

Beach fashions in the Venice / Ocean Park area.

Venice's Abbot Kinney Pier at night. The Auditorium is on the left, Ship Cafe in the center, and Dance Hall on the right.

with her at the pier's Ship Cafe. She left the next morning.

Ballroom dancing was an important social activity at any seaside resort at the turn of the century. Abbot Kinney, who wanted only the best, built at a cost of $40,000 one of the finest and largest dance hall on the Pacific coast. It opened on July 4th. It was huge, 190 x 210 feet, and could double as a convention hall when needed. Ten thousand people could fill the structure, and 800 couples could comfortably dance at one time. The finest orchestras played a variety of slow dances that were popular at the time.

Roller skating was another popular pastime that year, and during the fall became the rage in Southern California. Both the Venice and Ocean Park rinks were jammed nightly. Admission was ten cents and skate rental two bits. They featured exhibitions of championship skaters, Friday night races, and the new sport of roller polo.

Venice quickly fielded a team in the fledgling Southern California Roller Polo League. They were handicapped in their first game against Long Beach because the team used ordinary ball-bearing skates, whereas their opponents used pin-bearing skates that enabled them to run, jump and stop quickly. Seven hundred spectators watched Venice defeat Long Beach 2 - 0 in their first home game in October. Games were every Wednesday and Saturday nights and the local team made headlines by winning most of the time. But by Christmas, interest in the sport and roller skating in general wanned. Venice's first fad had ended.

The gracious Ship Cafe on the Abbot Kinney Pier was a replica of Juan Cabrillo's Spanish galleon.

Dance Pavilion on the Abbot Kinney Pier.

CHAPTER 2

Coney Island of the Pacific (1907-1912)

In the spring of 1907, Venice of America and Ocean Park, two sections of the city with opposing business interests were experiencing a series of muted differences. Neither the Marine Street businessmen led by G.M. Jones in Ocean Park, nor the Kinney people in Venice dared risk an open feud because it would be bad for business. The basic problem was that two rival communities were growing up in one municipality.

Venice in 1907 was part of the city of Ocean Park which had previously dis-incorporated from the city of Santa Monica several years before. The issue had been over differences in attitude among Santa Monica citizens dealing with gambling and serving alcoholic beverages in the Ocean Park pier district.

There was a power struggle going on between Kinney and Ocean Park's five man Board of Trustees, two of which were his ex-partners. At first their tactics were subtle; they provided less than adequate police, fire protection, and garbage collection in the Venice of America area. When the citizens passed a bond issue to finance the City Hall, Kinney offered several land parcels that would have been fairly central to the community. Instead the Trustees accepted a ten acre site offered by David Evans, a partner of Mayor Burke. The land was in Venice's outback, so far from everything that it would be later dubbed 'Tokio Palace' because the citizens perceived it about as far away as its namesake in the Orient. Despite an unofficial straw vote by the property owners in favor of an alternate site, the Trustees paid Evans $5000 for the property and awarded the building contract to a contractor in May.

Meanwhile Kinney noticed that the public was divided between his two amusement areas; the beach and pier on one hand, and the lagoon with its midway and bathhouse on the other. That spring he decided to consolidate these two areas on the beach.

When he applied for a construction permit for his bathhouse, the Board of Trustees refused to act. Several of them, who owned the Ocean Park Bathhouse a mile north of Windward Avenue, were accused of being afraid of the competition. Kinney, however, didn't wait. Venice was his town, so he proceeded with his plans. He ordered his men to pour the concrete foundation for his new bathhouse.

The Venice Plunge at Market Street on Ocean Front Walk was the largest heated salt-water pool on the west coast, 1908.

Aquarium on the Abbot Kinney Pier; 1908. (above)

Interior of the Venice Plunge with its hot salt-water fountain. (below)

The Trustees were infuriated. They immediately pulled the licenses for Kinney's tent city, and ordered it removed. His liquor licenses were revoked, dancing was banned in the pier ballroom, and Marshall G.G. Watt was instructed to remove the foundation of the bathhouse by whatever means possible.

The bath house foundation was scheduled for demolition by dynamite on Monday, June 10, 1907, a day when the beach crowds would be gone. Marshall Watt posted the necessary warning signs. But early that morning woman and children began arriving with picnic baskets. At 9:30 A.M. Watt ordered them to disperse - they didn't move. Soon more than 200 women, mostly from the Pick and Shovel Club, a civic club of which Mrs. Kinney was an ardent supporter, were picnicking on the uncompleted walls of the doomed bathhouse.

George Culver, city street superintendent, who was to perform the demolition, became more and more frustrated as the hours passed. At noon he gave up and returned to his office. Kinney, who never did get a permit, continued construction of his bathhouse and the city Trustees did not attempt to demolish it again.

The Trustees had badly miscalculated Kinney's intentions of retaining control of Venice of America. They knew that E.H. Harriman of the Los Angeles Pacific was negotiating to purchase the resort for $2.7 million, and they were certain that a little pressure would force Kinney to sell. Instead the incident focused attention on Jones' boss rule and the corrupt Board of Trustees.

Kinney's strategy was to dis-incorporate and elect a more agreeable set of Trustees. His petition for dis-incorporation of the city easily got more signatures that the number of voters in the last election.

With his tent city and dance hall closed down, and his inability to sell liquor at his Ship's Cafe and other eating establishments, Kinney decided to fight back economically. He temporarily shut down the rest of his operations, thereby depriving the city of a large share of its revenue. To compensate for lack of services, he organized his own private police and fire departments.

Despite some efforts to reconcile differences and the reopening of Kinney's businesses that summer, the dis-incorporation election was held on September 30, 1907. At first, Burke, Jones, and Robinson set the election for April 1908, about the time their terms were to run out, but fearing the outraged populace, they changed their minds and set the election sooner. The election was fought bitterly by both sides.

Ocean Park forces won a hollow victory. Although

Abbot Kinney Pier at Windward Avenue; 1910.

Ferris wheel was installed on the Venice Pier in 1911.

Kinney's supporter's were clearly dominant, 206 to 176, they couldn't muster the necessary two thirds majority to dis-incorporate. The city government began to fall apart shortly thereafter, as several Trustees resigned under duress for their involvement in police department corruption. Kinney got his revenge in the 1908 spring elections. His Good Government League candidates forced the remainder of the Ocean Park supported Trustees out of office and controlled the Board of Trustees in to the early 1920's.

It would be another three years, in another election, before voters would finally change the name of their city officially to Venice. By 1911, when Progressive Republicans amended state laws to equalize tax burdens between annexed and annexing municipalities, Kinney immediately sought to annex the Venice Peninsula and other outlying tracts, and change the name to Venice. Voters wholeheartedly backed his proposals on May 29, 1911.

Kinney was too preoccupied with politics in 1907 to devote much time to expansion of his amusement interests. He put an experienced Coney Island showman named Kavanagh in charge of the Midway Plaisance. He painted all the buildings white, and renamed it 'White City', a name often used for World's Fair style midways. Ten cents admission at the gate included free attractions and a concert by Placido Gilgi's sixteen piece band. The attractions included Leora's trapeze act, and Tarasca's daring bicycle ride in which he rode down a steep ramp to gain enough speed to leap through a circle of fire then across a 36 foot wide gap. In June 1907 'White City' almost burned down, but it was repaired and continued in operation through the 1908 summer season.

Work resumed on Kinney's $100,000 Venice Plunge in March 1908. The oceanfront bathhouse was huge. It contained 500 dressing rooms and a 150 x 100 foot hot salt water pool that could accomodate 2000 bathers. A wall of large glass windows gave the place a light, airy feel. Fresh salt water, filtered and changed three times daily cascaded from a fountain at one end. Twelve lifeguards were on duty on weekends to accomodate the crowds when it opened for summer business on June 21st.

The Aquarium was the first new attraction to debut on the Abbot Kinney Pier in January 1908. It exhibited the finest collection of marine specimens on the Pacific Coast. The central sunken seal and sea lion tank was surrounded by 48 glass tanks which contained live convict, devil and jelly fish among others. There was also a fish hatchery and curio store within the structure. It

The Rapids was an early 'Tunnel of Love' boat ride.

Hades attraction on the Venice Pier.

33

The Thompson or Venice Scenic Railroad built in 1910 along Ocean Front Walk next to the Venice Pier was an early roller coaster. It had mountainous scenery, two lift hills and a brakeman to slow down the cars on curves.

Venice beach in front of the Venice Plunge. The Venice Scenic Railroad is in the background; 1910.

Volunteer lifeguards launching a dory near the Venice Pier.

later became the official marine biological station for the University of Southern California.

They also began extending the pier 200 feet beyond the breakwater for fishermen that summer, and built a plaza and garden between the Auditorium and Dance Hall. It was modeled after the famous Continental Gardens in Philadelphia. It was also to be the last summer season for the lagoon midway. The freshly refurbished 'Rialto' had all new attractions and shows, but the public preferred to head directly for the beach when they embarked from the trolleys, and did not always stop at the midway before leaving for the day.

The decision to turn the pier into a full scale amusement zone site wasn't made until the following year when Kinney abandoned the lagoon midway concept entirely. Unfortunately there was no place to put the amusements on the beach since it had already been dedicated to the city with the provision that it could never be commercialized. All of the oceanfront lots had either been sold off or built upon. Kinney's only choice was to expand on Atlantic City's pier concept in a much bigger way.

In January 1910 the L.A. Thompson Company announced that they would construct a one and a half mile scenic railroad behind the dance hall and pavilion on the north side of the pier. It would have mountain terrain and tunnels with scenery in miniature. The three car electric trains would reach a point 65 feet above the waves before descending. A brakeman on the train would try to assure that the cars didn't derail on the turns, and a second lift hill gave customers their money's worth.

LaMarcus Thompson, a Sunday school teacher from Philadelphia, conceived this forerunner of the roller coaster as an alternate form of entertainment for the young people who often frequented beer gardens. After building a crude but popular unpowered device at Coney Island in 1884, he built the first fully developed roller coaster at Atlantic City two years later. It had gentle four foot dips and went only 5 - 10 MPH. He called it the Oriental Scenic Railroad because halfway through the ride the cars ducked into a dark tunnel where it tripped a light switch that revealed picturesque scenes of the Orient. The tunnel portion of the ride gave young couples a chance for a quick embrace and a kiss. Thrills plus intimacy became the two most important ingredients for a successful roller coaster.

Kinney added a number of small concessions at the inland end of the pier's south side. These included a Dentzel Carousel, a Hades attraction, an indoor

An unknown family poses for a photograph near the Abbot Kinney Pier. The Dippy Dips aerial ride is in the background; 1912.

View looking west across Trolley Way shows ornate structures at Windward and the Abbot Kinney Pier in the distance, 1912.

children's slide called Bump the Bumps, a Japanese Tea House and the Ocean Inn restaurant. The pier was also widened to eliminate congestion.

Meanwhile Alexander Fraser, Kinney's old partner, formed the Fraser Million-Dollar Pier Company. Their intent was to build the world's largest amusement pier in Ocean Park. It would be 285 feet wide, incorporate the existing pier and extend 1000 feet into the ocean. The pier alone without the buildings and concessions would cost $175,000. It would have a Dancing Pavilion, Revolving Cafe 110 feet in diameter, Thompson Scenic Railroad, Palace of Mysteries, Carousel, Mountain Roll Railroad, Trip to Mars, Vaudeville and Scenic Theaters. The grand opening would be June 1911.

They were serious this time. The contract was awarded July 29, 1910. Half the pier piles were in place by December, and they had extended the pier to almost 1500 feet. By the time the buildings were under construction the following February the payroll was running at $10,000 per week.

During the winter the Kinney Company competitively procured several new rides for their pier. A ferris wheel arrived from Seattle's Yukon-Pacific Exposition in January 1911 and workers began setting up the 45 ton ride at the western end of the Ship Cafe. Work was also progressing on the new 'Rapids' ride located on the pier at Windward. The contractor ordered an additional 250,000 board feet of lumber to complete the mammoth flume and water ride. Construction started on the 'Merry Widow' on the vacant lot at Windward and Ocean Front Walk, and the contract was awarded for the 'Automobile Races', a 160 foot diameter track ride located west of the ferris wheel.

The 'Rapids' opened Sunday, March 19th. It was an old mill style ride, in which fourteen foot long boats holding a dozen people wound their way through a 1510 foot serpentine canal. A large waterwheel near the entrance kept the water flowing. The walls at various sections of the ride depicted scenes like the Panama Canal, an Irish castle, and a view of the western frontier with a woman standing at the cabin door about to warn her husband of an approaching bear.

Later that month Fred Church and Frank Prior of Chicago announced that they would build their 'Giant Safety Racer', a racing roller coaster so huge that it would occupy the entire Midway Plaisance grounds. It would feature two trains racing on parallel tracks each measuring 4000 feet, and cost $61,000. The entrance would be on Trolleyway at Windward. Shortly thereafter, Fred Ingersol, a Chicago man, arrived to oversee construction.

The Race Thru the Clouds roller coaster was built along the south side of the lagoon and extended up Grand Canal. Boathouse is on right; 1911.

Cars raced two abreast along parallel tracks on the Race Thru the Clouds rollercoaster.

The Race Thru the clouds roller coaster drew long lines of paying customers. It was the first racing roller coaster built on the West Coast, and with each track 4000 feet long, it offered a long thrilling ride; 1911.

The two partners came out to Southern California to get on the ground floor of the amusement business. Prior, a natural showman, had been manager of Forest Park and later publicity director of Riverside Amusement Park. Church, who was the head engineer of a machine shop, manufactured parts for amusement rides. Their collaboration and sense of what the public wanted would produce new and innovative rides that would thrust Venice into the limelight as an important amusement center.

Ocean Park's Million-Dollar Pier was rapidly nearing completion. The L.A. Thompson Company, who had acquired the property south of the pier, was building the Dragon Gorge Scenic Railroad parallel to Ocean Front Walk. The building took up several blocks and contained several attractions like the 'Grotto Cafe', a revolving restaurant, and the 'Auto Maze'. The Looff family was building an ornate carousel in the Hippodrome building, on the site of the old Toboggan Railway between the Dragon Gorge and the Casino. It was a 50 foot diameter pit machine with horses four abreast.

The Grand Canyon Electric Railroad out on the pier was one of the first attractions to open. Its centerpiece was a 135 foot mountain peak with a waterfall at its summit. At night the electric lights gave it the appearance of an erupting volcano. The $100,000 ride built by Paul D. Housh had a third rail to power the four car trains around curves and up steep inclines. A motorman had control of the car's speed and often added unexpected thrills by powering down the hills as well as up. It is remarkable that there were no serious accidents as the cars often exceeded their safe speed limit on turns.

Apparently the builder wasn't initially satisfied with the attraction, for he began extensive renovation after it was open only one month. The ride turned out to be too short because of the high speed of the cars. In an attempt to make it the longest scenic railroad in the world, he added 2000 feet of additional track, put in nine more dips and a scenic tunnel. The new improved ride was nearly a mile in length.

Fraser's Million-Dollar Pier officially opened the weekend of June 17th, 1911. Tens of thousands attended the two day gala event. They danced in the huge ballroom at the end of the pier, watched vaudeville at the 1000 seat Starland Theater, or visited the pier's many rides, shows and exhibits. The 'Third Degree' advertised 'a smart show for smart people', when in reality it featured a moving sidewalk that transported people past snow and mountain scenery. There was a

Barnstorming pilots with their biplanes were popular at Venice Beach. Pilots often used the beach for a runway.

The Virginia Reel on the Venice Pier; 1912.

At the beach beside the Venice Pier; 1912.

Thompson Scenic Railroad along Ocean Front Walk near the Venice Pier; 1910.

Crooked House to explore, the City Jail to escape from and the Society Whirl. One of the more interesting exhibits was the 'Infant Incubators' which showed the latest in medical technology. Premature infants were given free care by trained nurses in an era when it wasn't readily available at local hospitals.

Additional attractions opened later that summer and into the fall season. Another hippodrome opened on the pier adjacent to the dance hall. It featured an ornate Philadelphia Toboggan Company carousel. The Mystic Maze and Panama Canal exhibit also found space on the pier.

The 'Race Thru the Clouds' roller coaster in Venice opened on July 4th, 1911. Church and Prior, the owners, did record business that day. The coaster, with only one half of the cars on line, carried 25,230 people from 8:30 A.M. to 1:15 A.M. It was the first racing roller coaster on the west coast, and it offered the public a long and thrilling coaster race ride with plenty of steep dips and speed. The long ess turn tunnel before the first incline proved to be very popular. The coaster got more than its share of repeat riders from a public that was looking for something new and exciting.

The ride was designed by John Miller, the inventor of the racing roller coaster and perhaps the most important and inovative coaster designer of all time. His inventions of the anti-rollback device on the lift hill, and the underwheel, an extra set of wheels beneath the track that prevented the car from jumping the track, led to the development of the high speed deep dip coaster.

Tom Prior, forever the showman, served a unique roller coaster dinner to twenty people that August. They ate the first course at the loading platform, went for a ride on the coaster, then ate the next course and rode again until the meal was finished (and/or they got sick).

The Merry Widow Waltz Trolley opened on Ocean Front Walk directly across from the pier in a small but elongated structure. It resembled the Rapids on the exterior but its cars ran on tracks instead of water. The seats were on movable bottoms. The car's swaying effect combined with its forward motion gave the ride a waltzing effect.

And workers a half a block south on Zephyr were preparing for opening of the Captive Balloon ride. The huge hydrogen filled gas balloon was to be held captive on a 1400 foot long cable. It would give customers wonderful views of Venice and its pier area. It worked fine until it escaped a year and a half later. The two passengers and pilot landed safely near Long Beach about twenty miles southeast.

Fraser's Million Dollar Pier featured, a dance hall, two scenic railroads, two carousels, a vaudeville theater, an auditorium, and numerous concessions; 1911.

Philadelphia Toboggan Company carousel on the Fraser Pier; 1912.

Ornate front of Thompson's Dragon Gorge Scenic Railroad; 1911.

Dance Pavilion on Fraser's Million Dollar Pier.

Night view shows both the Grand Canyon (foreground) and Dragon Gorge (background) Scenic Railroads, 1912.

The new Neptune Theater, an early nickelodeon, and the Merryland penny arcade opened for business on Ocean Front Walk across from the Thompson Scenic Railroad. By 1911 penny arcades were becoming amusement park mainstays. For a penny, people could drive slot cars, have their strength tested, or watch historical events in a hand cranked kinetoscopes. Couples could have the emotion of their kiss measured, and men could look at what at that time were considered rather erotic shots of women clad in bathing suits.

In October work was begun on the Johnson Captive Airplane ride on the Abbot Kinney pier. Plans were for a ten passenger airplane to travel on a cable track from the 114 feet high main tower at the inland end of the pier to three other smaller towers further out on the pier. The plane would board passengers on the ground, proceed up a spiral track to the top where it would be attached to the cable. It would then slide down along the cable to each of the smaller towers. While novel, it was poorly engineered and didn't give the public much of the thrill of riding an airplane. It eventually opened the following summer after the builders solved the problem with its heavy cars on slack cables nearly reaching the ocean waves. However, when another aerial ride, the Dippy Dips opened shortly afterwards on the opposite side of the pier, Captive Airplanes couldn't compete and closed only a year later.

That fall it began to look like the Ocean Park area would soon have two additional piers. Jones sued Fraser and won the franchise to build a small 400 feet by 100 foot pier next to the Million-Dollar Pier. He wanted Fraser to tear down the small portion of the pier on his side of the property line.

But the big news was Great Western Amusement Company's pier project across from the Decatur Hotel immediately south of Fraser's pier. Plans showed a pier 1000 feet long, 263 feet wide with a gigantic entrance arch 113 feet wide, 94 feet high and 60 feet deep. The Tivoli Cafe was to be on the south side of the arch in a 50 foot square tower, 135 feet high. A large 105 foot high racing roller coaster with 13,000 feet of track would occupy an area of nearly two acres. A casino, ferris wheel and several other concessions would be built on the remaining space, and at night 10,000 light bulbs would illuminate the entire pier. Work didn't start on the pilings until mid May 1912, and by then there was no rush to finish it for the coming summer season.

New ride construction on or adjacent to the Abbot Kinney Pier in Venice kept construction crews busy

Auditorium at Fraser's Million Dollar Pier; 1911.

Ocean Front Walk looking south near the entrance to the Fraser Pier in Ocean Park; 1912.

High up in the Mountains, Dragon Gorge. Ocean Park, Cal.

Along Ocean Front Walk just north of the Dragon Gorge Scenic Railroad; 1911.

Dragon Gorge Scenic Railroad car on a high turn; 1911.

Ocean Front Walk at the Fraser Pier. The Dragon Gorge, the large ornate structure with the towers, was an early roller coaster. The white hippodrome building in the center housed a Looff carousel. (opposite page)

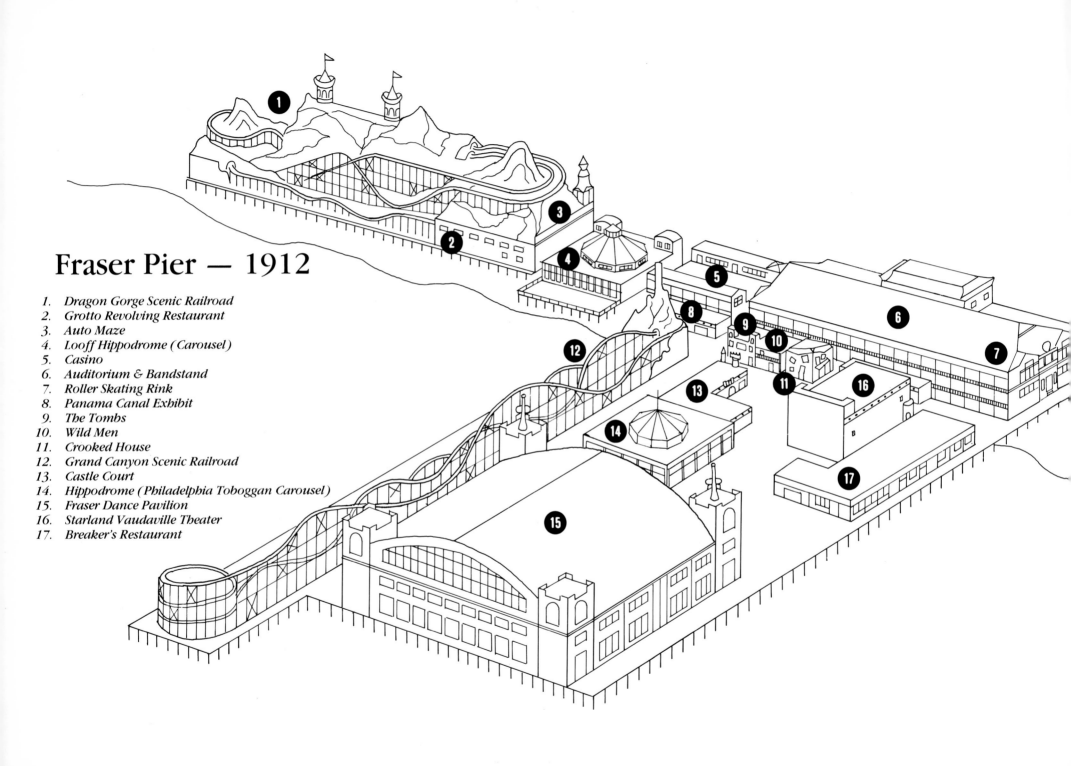

Fraser Pier — 1912

1. *Dragon Gorge Scenic Railroad*
2. *Grotto Revolving Restaurant*
3. *Auto Maze*
4. *Looff Hippodrome (Carousel)*
5. *Casino*
6. *Auditorium & Bandstand*
7. *Roller Skating Rink*
8. *Panama Canal Exhibit*
9. *The Tombs*
10. *Wild Men*
11. *Crooked House*
12. *Grand Canyon Scenic Railroad*
13. *Castle Court*
14. *Hippodrome (Philadelphia Toboggan Carousel)*
15. *Fraser Dance Pavilion*
16. *Starland Vaudaville Theater*
17. *Breaker's Restaurant*

*The Crooked House on the Fraser Pier was an early fun house.
Customers were challenged to escape from the Tombs; 1911.
(below left)
Castle Court on the Fraser Pier, 1911. (below right)
Electric tram service on Ocean Front Walk between
Venice and Ocean Park began operation in 1916.
(opposite page)*

throughout the spring of 1912. The circular 160 foot diameter 'Auto Races', delayed for nearly a year, began to take shape just beyond the Ship Cafe. It was designed like a merry-go-round, but the cars could pass. A large organ at front center provided the music. A new building across from the Dance Hall was built to house Ellis's Dentzel carousel which was already operating on the pier.

The Kinney Company procured a Virginia Reel ride from Henry Riehl, designer and superintendent of Luna Park in Coney Island. It was placed on the pier directly across from the Ship Cafe. Passengers riding in circular shaped cars on pivoted wheeled trucks descended from the top along a sloped serpentine track. Projections on the car's freely rotating body would cause it to spin when it engaged springs alongside the track. Near the end of the ride, the revolving tubs would spiral inward, then plunge down a steep drop at high speed into a darkened tunnel, plunging passengers into the unknown. It was a real thrill-seekers ride with sudden turns and spinning tubs that disoriented passengers.

Tom Prior built a miniature motordrome on the Windward property across from the St. Marks Hotel. A daredevil driver raced his car along the 65 degree walls of the high banked saucer shaped track six times daily. 'Dare Devil Race for Life' was a dangerous exhibit as

51

drivers would try to career around the track faster and faster until their wheels just touched the red danger line near the top of the track.

The first driver was involved in a freak accident only two days after the show opened. A crane was hoisting his car out of the bowl when it slipped and crushed him. Hal Shain took over and drove it until the end of the year, when on December 30th he opened the throttle a little too far. His car, going 55 MPH, went past the red line and smashed into the wooden guard rail. Splintered wooden timbers struck several spectators, while the demolished car rolled over and crashed into the center in a heap. The driver was rushed to the hospital but was dead on arrival. Bert Hall, a former mechanic, took over as driver four days later.

The Venice/Ocean Park area had become the finest amusement center on the west coast and was achieving fame as the 'Coney Island of the Pacific'. Besides the innovative rides, dance halls, theaters, plunges, and bowling alleys, there were dozens of places for a game of chance. Hype and innovation were the rule, and it was on the Venice Pier that Felix Simmonds, a concessionaire, claimed to have invented the hamburger. In 1912, the bathing beauty contest was started as a promotional feature for the Los Angeles Examiner newspaper.

Actually, any event or holiday was cause for celebration. Venice never failed to publicize them, for its economic base was primarily tourism and amusements. It was vital to the town's economy to attract large crowds on weekends and holidays. Visiting warships fired salutes offshore on Memorial Day, maypole dances were scheduled for the first of May, and colored eggs were passed out on Easter Sunday. Parades on all major holidays featured bands, floats, silent screen and sports celebrities. Special days were declared for any group or fraternal order that could guarantee a crowd.

Venice's hotel and amusement interests advertised heavily in newspapers and periodicals from Los Angeles to the East coast. In fact a large portion of winter hotel bookings came from the eastern states and Canada. Whenever an important convention was in Los Angeles, the delegates were invited to Venice. They were offered half price on amusements, and special aquatic events and band concerts were staged in their behalf. Elks, Shriners and other convention attendees never failed to spend at least one day on the pier.

Venice was, in those days, a place of wonder. It was a dream of genteel good fun come to life. There were events enough to satisfy everyone: dances at the pavilion, auto races, boxing matches, gondola excursions, ten

A Philadelphia Toboggan Carousel was installed in 1912 in the Hippodrome building on the Fraser Pier.

cent camel rides, and of course the attraction of sun, surf, and sand, even when heavy woolen bathing suits covered one completely.

On Saturday afternoons everyone dressed to the 'nine' for promenades on the boardwalk and gala events on the pier. Tourists could browse in the shops where they would find a wide selection of picture postcards, plaster of paris Italian statues, coral beads and mother of pearl necklaces. Outside on the piers and on Ocean Front Walk, vendors pushed little carts. "Hokey-Pokey's — two for five," they called. They sold little squares of ice cream. Others sold candied apples, endless twists of long pearly white salt water tafffy, clouds of pink cotton candy, strawberry phosphates, and cream puffs filled with custard. It was a place of smells, sounds and tastes, and hours of inexpensive fun for the visitor.

The Ocean Park amusement area seemed to be awash in new pier proposals when the Mountain Roll Company announced their plans in July 1912 to build yet another pier. This one was to be medium in size; 225 x 900 feet. An eight track mountain roll feature was planned as the main attraction and the remaining space to be used for concessions.

Jones and Fraser meanwhile continued their squabble until that summer the court finally ruled in Jones's favor. It seemed that when Jones and Fraser were partners there was a transfer of 100 feet of property, which had become the entrance of the Million-Dollar Pier. Jones claimed half of it, so the pier entrance would have to be cut in half. He could then build a larger pier, 150 x 400 feet.

Unfortunately, most of the new Ocean Park pier projects were prematurely derailed when fire broke out on Fraser's Million-Dollar Pier at 5 P.M. on September 3, 1912. Diners first noticed flames in the Casino restaurant. The cause was thought to be either a cigarette or a defective flue in the kitchen. A stiff shore breeze, fanning the flames, spread it quickly to other structures on the pier and to the buildings across Ocean Front Walk. Seven hundred firefighters from twelve municipal fire companies, some as far away as downtown Los Angeles, took three and one half hours to get the fire under control. The problem in fighting the fire was a lack of water pressure. They managed to stop the fire at the Ocean Park Bathhouse when the wind shifted to an offshore breeze.

The fire totally destroyed the pier, all of the amusements and six square blocks of businesses including many nerby hotels on Pier and Marine Streets. In all 225 structures burned. The loss was set at $3,000,000 with little of it covered by insurance. The business outlook for Ocean Park was bleak that fall, especially when Fraser, who was having a dispute with Santa Monica, talked of selling his beach property and moving out of town.

It looked like all of the entire beach amusement business would be in Venice during the next year, especially since Eddie Maier, the local brewery owner and William Stutzer, his contractor partner, had announced their plans for building a new amusement pier at Center Street, five blocks south of Kinney's pier. While they did announce their plans weeks before the Ocean Park fire, it looked even more viable with the lack of Ocean Park amusement competition.

Maier's plans called for a concrete pier 1300 feet long, the outer 1000 feet to be 550 feet wide. The pier would contain a huge plunge, a dance hall, a cafe in the shape of a sleek passenger liner, various rides and a children's Pavilion of Fun which would be free to children up to twelve. There would be parking for 700 automobiles at the base of the pier.

Work began on the pier pilings in November, but then abruptly stopped several weeks later. Rumors circulated that Maier suffered a business setback, while others thought he bought Fraser's beach property in Ocean Park.

The Fraser Pier fire on September 3, 1912 destroyed the entire pier and nearly all of Ocean Park's business district. The remains of the Looff carousel are in the left foreground.

CHAPTER 3

Growth Through the Teens (1913-1919)

Ocean Park businessmen were systematically rebuilding their burned out business district. New hotels, restaurants and shops began sprouting amidst the rubble. But the new amusement pier was on hold. The problem was that the city of Santa Monica was trying to gain control of Fraser's beach frontage at the foot of Pier Avenue, the proposed entrance of the new pier.

Fraser, who was discouraged and tired of fighting the city, was packed and ready to leave for Panama when local businessmen and bankers urged him to proceed with his new pier plans. He announced on January 25, 1913 that he would build a fireproof pier out of reinforced concrete, brick and steel. The entrance of the pier would be between Marine and Pier Avenues. It would be 285 feet wide and 1000 feet long, and it would be ready by May 15, 1913 for the summer season. The State Amusement Company, run by Ernest Pickering, signed a long term lease to operate the pier's amusements.

Meanwhile Eddie Maier and his associates, who were building the Center Street Pier in Venice, met in Los Angeles to adjust their differences. The delay was caused by a dispute between Maier and William Stutzer, the contractor. Stutzer demanded a fee of twenty percent of the pier cost, and expected to be furnished with all building materials at no cost. Maier thought his demands were exorbitant and refused. Delays continued through the spring and summer until Maier withdrew from the company in the fall. The remaining stockholders didn't have the money to complete the project.

Maier instead concentrated on bringing professional league baseball to Venice. He bought the Vernon franchise in the Pacific Coast League and moved the team to Washington Park in Venice for the 1913 season. The ballpark, which was on the southwest corner of what is now Venice and Washington Boulevards, was upgraded with a 4000 seat grandstand and 3000 bleacher seats.

The team, managed by "Hap" Hogan, consisted of older major league players and young hopefuls. Ex-major leaguers included Joe "Iron Man" McGinnity, Fred Harkness, John Kane, Dick Bayless, John Raleigh and Roy "Rinno" Hitt. The Tiger's first game on March 26, 1913 was an exhibition game with the Chicago

Automobiles and pedestrians cross a bridge over Coral Canal (now Main Street).

White Sox. Most of Venice attended the game in which the White Sox won 7 to 4.

The Tigers traveled up and down the coast to play opponents in Portland, Sacramento, Oakland, San Francisco and Los Angeles. After losing the opening double header against Los Angeles 3 to 2 in both games, they eventually finished third in the league with a 107-102 season record. The Tigers only played one more season in Venice, a fifth place finish with a 113-98 record.

In April Santa Monica filed an injunction to stop Fraser from building his pier. The city claimed that they owned 42 feet of ocean frontage at the foot of Pier Avenue, which in their eyes was merely an extension of the street. Fraser had previously given the city an easement to extend a sewer outfall there, but didn't deed them the land. Actually the injunction only prevented Fraser from building his pier entrance buildings adjacent to Ocean Front Walk. He was able to continue construction by setting the pier pilings further out than he had intended on the sand beyond the disputed property line.

The pier was rushed to completion and reopened on May 30, 1913. It was a much simpler design with a broad boardwalk running down the center of the pier. Various rides, booths and concessions were on either side. The pier, with its salt water fire prevention system using ten hydrants and a powerful steam pump, was supposed to be essentially fireproof.

Many of the attractions on the old pier were rebuilt. The 200 x 230 foot Dance Hall stood on the ocean end. Harry Hines directed his orchestra in the $50,000 structure. The bowling alleys and billiard hall were adjacent to it, and beyond them was the Rosemary Theater. A Parker carousel opened on the south side of the pier next to the Crazy House. Other attractions included the Breaker's Cafe, Crooked House, La Petite Theater, Roller Skating Rink, City Jail, Baby Incubators, Puzzletown and Mystic Maze. The pier lacked thrill rides its first season, but it did attract its share of tourist dollars.

There weren't many changes on the Abbot Kinney Pier in 1913, perhaps because Kinney felt that he already had better attractions than Ocean Park. Only the concession fronts on the south side of the pier from Hades to the Ship Cafe were refurbished. The Steeple-Chase Amusement Company leased space at the end of the pier for a giant four track Steeple-Chase and Derby Racing Coaster. They set up a demo booth on the pier to sell stock in their company at 85 cents per share. The

ride, if built, would feature a simulated horse race in which customers would ride mechanically driven horses along a gentle roller coaster style track.

Venice was crowded that summer with out of state tourists and tens of thousands of Los Angeles residents who commuted daily on the 'red cars'. Tragedy struck on July 13th when a three-car train, packed to the limit and outbound from Venice stopped near the Vineyard station because of stalled cars ahead on the track. Men with lanterns tried in vain to flag down the train behind coming up from Venice via the Short Line, but the forward car of the rear train crashed into the second train, telescoped its rear car and plowed right through its load of nearly 100 passengers. Twelve died and scores were injured - the town was shocked. Kinney immediately campaigned to have signal blocks installed on the track to prevent further tragedies.

Venice and Ocean Park businessmen were constantly campaigning for lower Pacific Electric trolley rates. Lower rates meant more visitors to their amusement districts. The Pacific Electric Company, although not always sympathetic, finally obliged and began offering special twenty-five cent half-fare days to the beach, mostly on summer Thursdays.

The Center Street pier owners were still quarreling when summer ended. What little they built of their pier was seriously damaged through carelessness when 200 feet of false work fell in the middle of the night in late September. The explosive sound of the pier's dynamo short circuiting as it fell into the sea caused the police to investigate for possible sabotage. By then Maier was fed up with his partner and offered to give the city all of his holdings in his pier company. The Trustees instead called his performance a breach of contract and granted a new franchise to Colonel August Stutzer to complete the pier at a cost of $75,000.

During the first week of January 1914 a vicious storm battered and damaged the Abbot Kinney Pier. The two wings over the breakwater were badly twisted and in danger of falling. The huge concrete pillars anchoring the Dippy Dip aerial ride were weakened, but the worst storm damage was along the beach south of the pier. Waves were breaking over the sidewalk, washing in as far as Speedway Alley and threatening beachfront homes. Several houses were destroyed and one-half mile of sidewalks were washed away.

The problem was that Venice had a badly eroding beachfront south of the pier. Of course Kinney never realized that by constructing a breakwater to protect his pier in 1905, it would divert currents in such a way that

a rapid narrowing and coarsening of the sand would result. The wide, fine-sand beach, advertised as 'the world's safest beach' because of water that was shallow several hundred yards from shore, changed dramatically.

It was becoming evident that Venice wasn't properly engineered, especially in the canals. Although the concept of Venice's canal system was sound, tidal flow through one narrow outlet to the sea failed to circulate the water properly through the miles of shallow dirt-walled canals. Two pipes under Windward and the pier, which usually supplanted the tidal flow, filled with silt and were often out of commission. When the flood gates at Playa del Rey silted up in April 1913 and the canals could only get fresh water when six foot high tides occurred, the State Board of Health condemned them as a menace to public health.

Other engineering mistakes included a sewage plant so overtaxed that sewage was discharged before it had time to ferment to harmless waste and a high pressure sea water fire protection that failed to work. The citizens repeatedly failed to pass needed bonds issues to repair them.

A new round of competition between the two pier areas occurred during spring 1914. Fraser won his court case against the city of Santa Monica, and was now able to build at his pier entrance at Ocean Front Walk. He decided to go ahead and rebuild the Casino.

Promoters managed to successfully raise the capital to begin construction of the Ben Hur Racer on the north side of his pier. The three-in-one project contained a big racing roller coaster designed by William Labb, a 7000 seat bandstand on a broad plaza and a 56 foot diameter carousel within the structure. An immense electric sign with the picture of Ben Hur driving a chariot adorned the top of the bandstand. The coaster was 75 feet high, 4200 feet in length and extended 700 feet over the ocean. It took much longer to build than expected, but it did manage to begin operation in late summer.

The Stepple Chase promoters decided to build their new ride on an extension of the Great Western Amusement Pier between Marine and Navy Streets instead of the Abbot Kinney Pier. Their company was capitalized at $200,000. A steam hammer for driving the piles was engaged and lumber was ordered from the northwest in hopes of completing the project by the end of the year. But the huge ride was never built, apparently because the promoters were unable to sell enough stock in their company.

The Kinney Company spent $100,000 in improvements to the Venice Pier during the spring and summer.

The view north from the top of the Race Thru the Clouds roller coaster shows the lagoon and canal area of Venice of America. Coral Canal is in the center (now Main Street) extends directly north; the old bathhouse building used as a high school until 1914 is to its left. Lion Canal with its bridge and Tent City is to the right, and Grand Canal is in the foreground on the far right; 1913.

CITY OF VENICE.
LOS ANGELES CO. CAL. 1913.

Most noteworthy was the addition of an automobile parking lot on the pier's south side. Seven hundred cars entering from Loreli Avenue could park for free. In addition they added a new life saving house and a wireless station for the weather bureau on the end of the pier. Kinney scored a major coup when Ernest Pickering, formerly head of the State Investment Company in Ocean Park, joined them.

Concessionaires, spending freely that year, added an Ostrich Farm across from the Dance Hall, a Zoological Garden at the end of the pier, a circular swing behind the Plunge, an Underground Chinatown exhibit in the bandstand tower and a cyclorama show called the Last Days of Pompeii. The skating rink, which was built on the site of the old auto ride, kept the hole in the center. It was extremely popular with visiting sailors who watched the surf as they skated around the oval rink. And the docks at the end of the pier serviced a 350 passenger boat that took tourists on a five mile excursion around Santa Monica Bay.

Kinney spent large sums of money for entertainment to attract people to his pier. He often hired aviators like Frank Sites to perform aerial stunts over the pier with his bi-plane. In May 1914 20,000 people watched him take off from the beach just north of the pier, when his passenger William Morton parachuted from 2500 feet and intending to aim for the beach, missed and landed unharmed in the water. Sites continued the show by doing daring dives and spiral drops towards the sea below.

Other barnstormers like Al Wilson, Frank Clark and Mort Bach performed regularly in the skies over Venice. Venice's own airport at the corner of Venice and Washington Boulevards became the first airfield on the west coast to be officially designated as an airport in 1914 thanks to Ince's Trans-Pac race.

Ince Field was established as a base for stunt pilots employed by the Abbot Kinney Company to entertain beach crowds and for movie work at nearby Inceville in Santa Monica Canyon. Some of the most daring and elaborate aerial stunts were dreamed up in the field's hangers and motion picture cameramen were often on hand to film them. Kinney had invited the aviation industry to town because he knew it would be a constant source of publicity.

The airport also supported a fledgling aircraft industry. Manufacturers like Fiske, B.H. Delay, Crawford Aircraft and Waterman Aircraft had small factories there. The airport was closed in 1923 after the land was subdivided.

Windward Avenue in 1913 was mostly undeveloped on the south side of the street. Two attractions, Dare Devil Race for Life and the Merry Widow occupied the block between Speedway and Ocean Front Walk.

Venice City Hall was built in 1907. (above)

Venice's first grammar school was Central School on Washington Boulevard at Westminster. (above right)

Villa City provided inexpensive accomodations for visitors. It was located south of Grand Canal and lasted until 1926. (left)

Ship Cafe on the Venice Pier is decorated with flags.

Electric tram service on Ocean Front Walk between Venice and Ocean Park began operation in 1916. (opposite page)

The public was so fascinated by aviation that they scheduled a balloon race on Sunday July 18, 1914. Only five of these highly flammable hydrogen balloons entered the long distance race. The winner would be the balloon that went the farthest.

The race was won by Ed Unger, whose large 72,000 cubic foot balloon 'California', carrying the pilot and a woman passenger, landed safely in Anaheim. The 'Fairy' the smallest of the balloons (15,000 cu. ft.), came in second. Although it could barely carry a pilot, it did make it to Long Beach. The airship 'Venice' came in third.

Venice's fascination with new forms of transportation extended to the automobile as well. Road racing, the most exciting spectator sport of the era, captured the public's fancy and also that of the Board of Trustees, who authorized the 1915 Venice Grand Prix on the streets of Venice. It was roughly a triangle course down Electric Avenue, Rose Avenue, and Compton Road (Lincoln Boulevard). The curves were banked for high speed turns. Eight thousand dollars in prize money was offered.

A Saturday afternoon St. Patrick's Day crowd of 75,000 watched the 300 mile road race from the bleachers and anywhere they could find a view. Seventeen drivers entered some of the fastest racing machines of their day; Bugatti, Simplex, Stutz, Mercer, Peugeot, Maxwell, Napier, Chevrolet, DeLage and Hercules. Mechanical problems plagued most of the drivers as one after another dropped out of the grueling race. Dave Lewis was in the lead on the 80th lap with just 17 laps to go when engine trouble forced him out of the race. Barney Oldfield's Maxwell went on to an easy victory. Billy Carlson, also driving a Maxwell, finished second just 41 seconds behind Oldfield. Only eight of the seventeen entries finished the race. Average speed of the winner in the four and one-half hour race was 68.5 MPH.

The race was considered a success despite injuries to bystanders when a scoreboard toppled, and the death of an elderly spectator who wandered on to the course and was struck by a car. However, the city lost $10,000 due to gate crashing and the sale of 1000 counterfeit tickets by con men. Despite 40,000 paid admissions, thousands rushed the gates and sneaked in when ticket takers were unable to handle the large crowd.

Nature wasn't very kind to Venice that winter and spring as a severe winter storm, much worse that of the previous year, severely damaged the pier and south beaches. Waves washed across Speedway as far inland as

Trolley Way. The extreme end of the Venice Pier was washed away, and thousands of spectators came to view a beach strewn with debris. The pier was closed beyond the Auditorium and weakened pilings under the Carousel opposite the Dance Hall caused it to close also. Naturally they began rebuilding immediately.

The annual bathing suit parade was scheduled for May 2nd. Several woman's clubs objected that it was "injurious to the community both from a material and moral standpoint." They suggested some standards for both women and men. Things became ridiculous when men were ordered from the beach for wearing one piece sleeveless suits that were just becoming fashionable. Bathers, who were afraid to go on the beach, threatened to go north to Santa Monica's less strict beaches.

The Trustees decided on some minimum regulations: for woman, skin fitting one piece suits ending in a skirt, the hem of which was considerably above the knees, suit high in front and back, with short sleeves and trunks of same length as skirt invisibly attached at waist, and stockings; for men, suit cut high under arms and in front and back, trunks embellished with a four inch skirt.

Venita Walker, one of the finest swimmers and divers on the west coast, was discovered and hauled before the censors for inspection. The suit, after some discussion, passed muster, but the bare legs - that would never do in Venice.

Miss Walker protested vehemently that she could never swim with a pair of nasty stockings dangling around her feet. Mayor Gerety was selected as arbitrator.

"A nice silk stocking on a nice plump leg always appealed to my esthetic temperament", he offered as an opinion, "but I must say that personally, I wouldn't care to go swimming with a pair of socks on - myself that is."

Although they modified the dress code to exclude stockings, bathers weren't thrilled with the prospect of being called out of the water for inspection on subsequent Sundays.

Venice was beginning to play an important part in the motion picture business which was quick to take advantage of the town's unique architecture and colorful amusement district. Nearby studios like Biograph and Bison in Santa Monica and the Ince Studio in Culver City sent film crews to Venice. Charlie Chaplin starred in the "Kid at the Auto Races", while Mary Pickford and Harold Llyod each played the lead in movies along the Venice canals. Movie companies became so numerous and disruptive to local business

The Venice Scenic Railroad was modernized in 1914 and its ornate mountain scenery removed.

The Great American Racing Derby on the Venice Pier was a horse racing style carousel where riders raced four abreast and each winner received a free ride, 1918. (above)

The Whip opened on the north side of the Abbot Kinney Pier in 1918. (below)

that for a time in 1915 there was talk of banning them. However no action was taken and in later years movies like "The Camera Man" starring Buster Keaton and several "Our Gang" comedies" were filmed along the beach front and on the pier.

The tourists not only enjoyed seeing their favorite stars in person, either making films on the streets or as patrons at local restaurants and hotels, but loved to watch their films. The Venice / Ocean Park area had four permanent movie theaters: the California and Neptune Theaters on Ocean Front Walk near Windward, and the Dome and Rosemary Theaters on the Ocean Park Pier. Also, Venice's large auditorium on the pier was often used to show movies. Sound from its fine organ was a welcome addition to those silent films. Admission then was ten cents for all seats, although some theaters charged only a nickel for children.

When the Panama Pacific Exposition in San Francisco closed in the fall, Kinney agents negotiate with

"Merryland" and Neptune Theatre, Venice, Cal.

Merryland Arcade and the Neptune Theater on Ocean Front Walk at Market Street; 1913. (above)

This ornate Dentzel Carousel was operated by J. A. Ellis on the Venice Pier; 1915.

exhibitors to bring 'Captain - the horse with human brains' to Venice. It was alleged to understand every word spoken to it and it performed tricks of addition, subtraction and multiplication. The horse was blindfolded so that hand signals couldn't be used to prompt it. The act opened on the pier where the old 'Bump the Bumps' stood. An alligator farm was also added that winter, and there were foolish plans to construct a 200 room hotel on the pier just beyond the Auditorium.

Ocean Park amusement interests suffered another setback that winter when a fire broke out in the Dance Pavilion on the Ocean Park Pier at 1 A.M. just as Christmas ended. The night watchman discovered the blaze in the check room and immediately called for help. The fire, fanned by a slight sea breeze, began its march up the pier. It consumed the Pioneer Bowling Alleys, Eskimo Village, Paris by Night, numerous small concessions and half the lofty Ben Hur Coaster before the combined fire brigades of three beach cities stopped it behind the Rosemary Theater. One-third of the pier was in ruins. The water-soaked Indian Village survived, but its merchandise was stolen when it was put out on the pier sidewalk.

The origin of the fire was thought to be arson. A concessionaire saw two men in a boat rowing away from the pier shortly before the blaze spread, but nothing was ever proven. When the firemen were cleaning up, they pulled down some of the Japanese gambling game wheels and found intricate electric wiring on the under side of the spindles. The games were rigged!

The first priority of the State Investment Company, operators of the Fraser Pier, was to build a temporary dance hall. Dance halls were more essential to nearby business interests than most people realized. Once their small 60 x 80 foot hall opened on February 12th, 1916, other business' receipts improved dramatically.

However, the company had much more ambitious plans. Obtaining the lease on the Jones Pier gave them control of 500 feet of beach frontage. They planned to rebuild the pier, erect a big first class cafe at the northwest corner of Ocean Front Walk and the pier entrance, add a big parking lot similar to the one on the Abbot Kinney Pier, and obtain the '33rd Degree' and the huge 'Aeroscope' attractions from the San Francisco Exposition if they could be moved.

By April work on their new concrete dance hall near the end of the pier was nearing completion, and it looked like they would make the Easter Sunday opening. H. W. Schlueler leased space on the Great Western Pier at Ocean Front Walk. He razed the Pier Athletic Club where many famous boxers trained and the adjacent shooting gallery to make space for a 165 foot square building. It would be part dance hall and part concert hall. The dance hall section would be under an enormous 100 foot diameter concrete dome.

Tom Prior and Fred Church leased space on Ocean Front Walk between the Fraser Pier's two entrances. They planned to introduce a new concept in amusement park rides, a racing carousel. They called their ride the 'Great American Racing Derby'. The inside portion of the ride was a standard carousel with 62 jumping horses and menagerie animals. However, on the outside rim of the 72 foot diameter machine were forty racing horses grouped four abreast in ten distinct races. The horses, which were set in six foot long tracks, would move back and forth as the ride rotated, sometimes nosing ahead to gain the lead, other times suddenly falling back. The ride would slowly gain speed until it reached 25-30 MPH, then the bell signifying victory for each of the lead horses would ring and the ride would slow down to a stop. The winners of each race would receive free repeat rides.

It was impossible to determine ahead of time which horse would win since the cables that moved the horses back and forth criss-crossed beneath the platform. The cable pulling the outside horse in one row might be pulling the second horse out in the row ahead. A 'Danger' sign restricted the ride to older children, but it was very popular among young jockeys, even at an expensive 15 cents for the one mile race.

Prior and Church originally scheduled the ride to open July 4th 1916, but delays in manufacturing the custom horses at the Parker factory in Leavenworth, Kansas prevented completion until Feb 4, 1917. Their instinct that the public was in love with racing proved correct, and they began manufacturing them for other amusement parks throughout the country.

The Dome Dance Pavilion, however did open open on time for the Fourth of July weekend. Ben Laietsky's Orchestra provided the music. The dance hall did record business on July 4th. 34,000 tickets were sold at five cents each to 68,000 dancers during the all day and evening dance sessions. Dance sessions in those days were usually three slow numbers long; combinations of fox-trots, one-steps and waltzes. When it was over they would clear the floor for a new group. In the evening Tex La Gronge entertained pier spectators with a thrilling daredevil aerial show surrounded by fireworks.

William H. Labb, frustrated with efforts to rebuild his

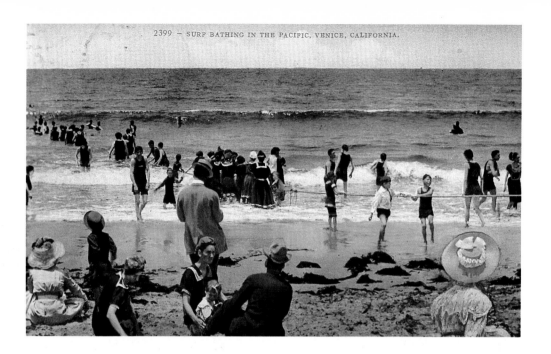

Bathers in the surf at the Venice Pier. The life lines at the left were to help those who couldn't swim from being knocked down by the surf.

The Venice Dance Hall was reserved for children on Saturday afternoons.

Ben Hur Racer, turned his attention to leasing the Great Western Amusement Company property in March 1917. He planned to turn the Dome Dance Pavilion into a Hippodrome for fun making devices. It would be a facsimile of George E. Tillyou's building at Steeplechase Park Coney Island, and would feature 57 varieties of fun and amusement devices under one roof. He also planned to have Chute the Chutes, Over and Under the Sea, a Blue Streak coaster, 33rd Degree, and a vaudeville theater all on an 800 foot pier. Unfortunately he was a better talker than money raiser and his plans were never implemented, at least that season.

Venice's summer was marred by an unfortunate accident at the Zoological Garden at the end of the pier. Children often fed food to the dangerous animals through the cage bars. A little girl, who tried feeding an ice cream cone to a bear, was caught, severely mauled, and killed. The bear was immediately disposed of.

Venice was a carefree, happy place and prospered well until the Europeans began squabbling and the United States was forced into fighting the Great War on April 6, 1917. The city was patriotic and that summer the Chamber of Commerce held Liberty Bond and Thrift Stamp Drives while parades to defeat the Kaiser marched along Ocean Front Walk. The first Westside volunteer soldiers, led by Sherwood Kinney, Abbot's son, received a big sendoff when they departed September 5th. Even Abbot Kinney, in a gesture of patriotic duty, petitioned the Navy to build a harbor at Playa del Rey for an anti-submarine fleet. Venice's aviation school contributed by training pilots for the war, and Crawford and Saunders were building war planes.

The onset of war meant that people would have to make sacrifices. The food conservator for the Venice area, in a meeting with restaurant owners, food vendors and saloon keepers, established a limit of two hot dogs per customer and banned the sale of sandwiches in saloons after 5 P.M. To conserve wheat and sugar, spaghetti was stricken from the menus and soft drinks were made less sweet. They eventually instituted meatless Tuesdays and wheatless Wednesdays, and rationed sugar one week each month. Ed Dunnivant, owner of the Ocean Inn was arrested shortly afterwards for hoarding sugar.

The Venice Vigilance Committee was formed and sought out anyone making disloyal remarks. Sometimes they were over-zealous and harassed shopkeepers of Germanic origin. Slackers and idlers, also considered disloyal, were picked up in periodic raids on the pier.

Main promenade on the rebuilt Fraser Pier; 1913.

Grand opening of the Ben Hur Racer roller coaster in Ocean Park; 1914.

Entrance to the Race Thru the Clouds roller coaster.

Underground Chinatown in the bandstand structure at the Venice Pier; 1914.

Boating on the canals at Coral Canal and the central lagoon; 1913

The brisk liquor sales along Windward Avenue were a sore point with prohibitionists because Venice was almost the only place in the vicinity of Los Angeles where drinking was still legal. Civic associations considered alcoholic beverages immoral and un-patriotic. Although it was illegal to sell alcohol to soldiers and sailors in uniform, Venice cafes and nightclubs did so regularly. In an attempt to stop this the Los Angeles County Board of Supervisors passed a resolution asking the federal government to close liquor stores and saloons completely.

Nearby Santa Monica voted to go 'dry' on January 1, 1918. Venice's election on the liquor laws was to be that April. Both sides were campaigning for their cause, sometimes fighting unfairly. Just days before the election the Grand Jury began to dig into alleged fraud and false voter registration in Venice. It was an open secret that almost anyone who would vote 'wet' could obtain free lodgings in Venice. Some Santa Monica bartenders moved there with the promise of free house rent for 6 months. The 'wets' carried the April 7th election by 509 votes. Venice and Vernon were now the only places in Los Angeles County where one could buy a drink or a bottle of liquor.

The war effort did little to restrict additions in the amusement zone. Church-Prior installed another Great American Racing Derby on the Venice Pier between the Auditorium and Melodia. It was a larger machine, 315 feet in circumference with 64 horses in rows of four set on the racing rim. It was a much more efficient design with no inner carousel. The outdoor ride set up under a tent was an immediate success.

Tom Prior, who operated the business, seemed to be at odds with the politicians in both Venice and Santa Monica. When the Trustees insisted that he cease playing his Race Thru the Clouds calliope, he severed relations. He scheduled a religious music concert one month later to prove to his foes that his calliope could play reverent and subtle music.

He also sued the city of Santa Monica for unreim-bursed expenses incurred in the building of a bandstand in conjunction with his Racing Derby on the Ocean Park Pier. In January 1918 he removed the ride from the pier and attempted to demolish the building. Fraser called in the police to stop him. Prior claimed that Santa Monica's restrictions, particularly those against games of chance, were bad for business. This was hard to fathom since just the previous season his ride had 211,993 customers during the period from June 1 to Sept 16.

The Whip also opened that season on the Abbot Kinney Pier just above the Virginia Reel. Its cars traveled in a straight line, then made a swift half circle turn at each end. It was owned by Crandell, who also operated the Scenic Railroad. Over the years he had improved his coaster by adding more dips to make the ride even more daring.

W. H. Labb and William Ellison, trying for success one last time, took over the management of the Fraser Pier. Once again they had ambitious plans for construction of a Shoot the Shoot ride, Fun Palace, Under and Over the Sea, and a Carousel in the area on the north side of the pier where the old Ben Hur Racer stood. The war delayed their plans as it did construction of the Dragon Baths proposed on the old Dragon Gorge site along Ocean Front Walk.

When the Armistice was signed November 11, 1918, California was in the midst of a killer influenza epidemic. At first the flu epidemic wasn't feared, for county health officials like Dr. J. L. Pomeroy were certain that Southern California's sunshine would prevent it. But by late October the flu spread and the health department overseeing Venice and Santa Monica was forced to close schools, theaters, saloons and all places where soft drinks and ice cream were sold. The latter places had to establish a sanitation and sterilization system for glasses before they were allowed to reopen. Regulations were quirky and often silly. Music and liquor were allowed in restaurants, but no dancing. Bars and saloons had to shut down but not package liquor stores.

At first the flu seemed to spare Venice. Perhaps washing down the streets with salt water did the trick, or due to the lack of medical facilities the afflicted just went elsewhere. Regardless, Venice was well enough to lift the quarantine for the Armistice Day celebration. Only one dance hall and two theaters were closed, while nearby Santa Monica was shut down tight. Everyone thought the epidemic was over when an alarming increase occurred - 169 new cases and six deaths were reported the week of December 12th. Everyone wore flu masks on the streets, and the flu bandits were having a splendid time robbing businesses. The influenza epidemic was still around but abating by the end of January 1919.

On April 3, 1919 Venice inaugurated the first aerial police force in the United States by swearing in aviator Otto Meyerhoffer into the police force. The words 'Venice Aero Police' were inscribed in big bold letters on the side of his 100 MPH biplane. The police station would call him at the airport when they needed his assistance in tracking fleeing automobile bandits into the mountains, or finding boats in distress.

The amusement industry, relieved that the war and flu epidemic were finally over, proceeded with plans for expansion and change that spring. The Kinney Company enlarged their pier from the Auditorium to the north wing of the tee and planned to put amusement attrac-tions there. They added an indoor tunnel of love ride called 'Over the Falls' next to the 'Oriental Gardens' at the end of the pier. It featured boats inside that swooshed down a four foot high sloped chute then glided past a scenic waterfall. Next to it a new fun house called 'Smiles', and later renamed 'Hellarity Hall' was opened. And a new Cafeteria situated between the Dance Hall and bowling alleys did extremely well, serving 2500 meals per day. A barker with a megaphone lured customers inside by shouting, "This is a nice place to eat when you are hungry."

That summer the district attorney clamped down on all the so called 'games of chance' in both pier districts. It affected all those games where a prize was given, but not amusement games where admission was charged like skee ball and bowling. While there had been previous crackdowns on gambling style games, this time it looked like the games would have to change to those involving skill only. Naturally it affected business. Many people, especially adults, enjoyed the games more than the thrill rides.

In Ocean Park concessionaires were becoming extremely unhappy with pier management. They and the local business owners demanded that Labb and Ellison advertise, put in real attractions and decent entertainment on the pier. The American conces-sionaires felt that the Japanese concessionaires were getting a better deal. They didn't have to wait long. Ernest Pickering purchased the Fraser Million-Dollar Pier on July 2, 1919. He left immediately on a tour of East coast amusement parks to procure the newest and best rides for his pier. For the time being, the only imminent change was the Rosemary Theater's move into the old Racing Derby building along Ocean Front Walk. Improvements would have to wait untill Pickering returned in the fall.

CHAPTER 4

Setbacks, Rebuilding, & Political Confusion (1920-1924)

The year 1920 would prove to be pivotal for Venice and its amusement industry. It was a time when Venice's popularity as an amusement center began to wane. Radio, motion pictures and the widespread ownership of automobiles began to compete for entertainment dollars.

The cyclical pattern marked by seemingly endless summers of prosperity and growth followed by winters of hard times and empty streets was ending. Venice was maturing at a time when summer attendance was declining. Visitors became residents who stayed year-round to raise families, and Venice provided for their needs. The city, servicing a permanent population of 10,385, had one of the better school systems in the area: four grammar schools and a combined junior-senior high school. There were several Protestant and Catholic churches in Venice, and the city had two influential newspapers, the Venice Vanguard and Venice News.

Financial problems, however, began to plague the municipal government as prohibition coupled with a drop in visitor attendance cut city revenues. Once Congress passed the Volstead Act prohibiting the sale and consumption of alcoholic beverages, the states quickly ratified the 18th amendment to the United States Constitution in 1919. Prohibition took effect one year later at midnight January 16, 1920.

Many of the area's drinking establishments and high class restaurants either changed hands or went out of business. Those in the Windward business district included four of the best saloons west of the Mississippi. The 'First & Last Chance Bar', 'Menotti's', 'Decatur', and the 'Mecca Buffet' helped Venice become the finest amusement center in the west. The revenue from their $300 per month liquor licenses helped build Venice Union Polytechnic High School. Now Menotti's was to become a grocery store, the Strand Cafe an ice cream parlor and lunch room, and the Mecca Buffet a drug store.

Tax revenue was severely cut. The city had previously collected $138,000 annually from taxes and business licenses, plus an additional $30,000 from liquor licenses. Earlier debts dating back as far as storm damages in 1914 had been mostly carried as bonds totalling $80,000. While this was a paltry sum in comparsion to other city's bond indebtedness, Venice was financially in trouble now that they lost the revenue from liquor licenses.

Entrance to the Abbot Kinney Pier; 1920.

Max Senett Keystone Company movie star parade along Ocean Front Walk in Venice.

V. 29.   Dance Pavilion on the Pier,
Venice, California.

Dance Pavilion on the rebuilt Venice Pier; 1921.

Lick's Dome Pier, Ocean Park, Calif.

Lick Pier in Ocean Park; 1922.

V. 27.   Concessions on the Pier.
Venice, California.

Venice Pier midway on the rebuilt pier; 1921.

Some of the Amusements on the Pier, Ocean Park, California.

Frolic ride on the Pickering Pier in Ocean Park; 1920.

Still, amusement people were optimistic. Ocean Park Pier owner, Fredrick Pickering, and amusement ride designers Fred Church and Frank Prior, who took over after his father's death, were planning big things for the 'Coney Island of the Pacific Coast'. The latter two were razing the old 'Rapids' ride to make space for a new roller coaster designed by John A. Miller. The innovative 70 foot high 'Big Dipper' featured dips on the curves as well as the straight-aways. It opened May 8th, 1920. They were also building a ride called the 'Mill Chutes' that combined the old mill style tunnel of love ride with a water toboggan slide at the end. The boats would float through tunnels, some historic, some fairyland, until they reached the incline where they would be hauled up by a chain over a huge water wheel to descend into a large lagoon below. Its entrance was on the Ocean Front Walk, only twenty feet from the pier entrance.

Leonard Crandell was busy razing his Scenic Railroad and planned to move it to Ocea Park. The 1500 seat California Theater was to be built on the former coaster site. New attractions near the end of the pier included the Bug House, an illusion ride where one sat in a swinging chair that appeared to swing higher and higher. In reality the walls rocked back and forth, higher and higher, until the room turned upside down around the nearly stationary customers. With the nearby Pig Slide the player had to throw a ball through a circular hole to start the animal performers. The little pigs that were released from their pens slid down an incline and were then herded back to their pens by a trained fox terrier. In addition, a Noah's Ark attraction depicting the biblical story opened near the pier entrance.

Construction began in March on the expansion of Ocean Park's Pickering Pier and the addition of five exciting new rides. Pickering, in an attempt at one-upsmanship over Venice, was doubling the size of his pier to 400,000 square feet. It would be the largest pier in the world. As a comparison Venice's pier had about 250,000 square feet of space, and Atlantic City's pier only 75,000 square feet. Investors could buy shares of stock in his company.

Crandell decided to design and build a brand new racing roller coaster on the old Ben Hur site instead of reconstructing his outdated scenic railroad. His new Blarney Racer wasn't a very fast ride, and unfortunately never did make its money back. It shared the site with a Ye Old Red Mill ride whose course ran under the arches of the racing coaster. Its boats ran part way in the open, reminiscent of a mountain stream. On the far end of the site was a rather unique attraction, the Monkey Speedway Auto Races. It was a game in which monkeys would

Dentzel Carousel on the Pickering Pier in Ocean Park; 1920.

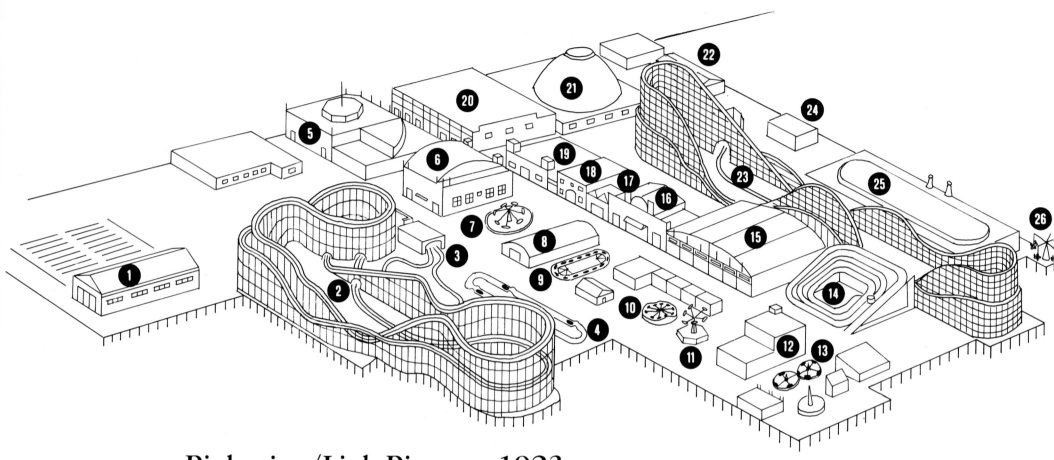

Pickering/Lick Piers — 1923

1. Ocean Park Municipal Auditorium
2. Blarney Racer Roller Coaster
3. Old Mill
4. Witching Waves
5. Rosemary Theater
6. Merry-go-round (Dentzel)
7. Frolic
8. Dodge 'em
9. Whip
10. Caterpillar
11. Captive Aeroplanes
12. Over the Rockies
13. Double Whirl
14. Over the Top
15. Crackerbox Dance Hall
16. Skeeball
17. Puzzletown
18. Strand Theater
19. Breaker's Restaurant
20. Billiards & Bowling
21. Dome Theater
22. Dodge 'em
23. Zip Roller Coaster
24. Skee Ball
25. Bon Ton Ballroom
26. Captive Aeroplanes

Blarney Racer roller coaster at the Pickering Pier; 1920. (left)

Aerial view of the Pickering Pier in Ocean Park looking north; 1920. (below)

peddle miniature autos along three tracks and people could bet on the winner of the each race.

Pickering rebuilt and enlarged the pier's dance hall and placed new rides around it. The Captive Aeroplane and Tango rides were built directly opposite the Crackerbox Dance Hall. Over the Top, a big hit at Luna Park in Coney Island, was installed by Henry Riehl in the area west of the dance hall. It was a cross between a Virginia Reel and a small spiral coaster. The rotating saucer shaped cars, traveling up, over, and down the 30 degree slope, steadily spiraled inward until they exited through a tunnel to the outer loop's station.

The 'Frolic' ride was placed directly across from the 'Ye Old Red Mill'. Twenty four people rode chariots that whirled around a circle 200 feet in circumference. The chariots tipped forward and backwards at a 45 degree angle, and swayed outwards with centrifugal force.

William Dentzel's beautiful 72 animal 'Carousell' occupied an 80 foot square building between the Frolic and the new Rosemary Theater. This Philadelphia made ride along with its mechanical organ cost $22,500. Other attractions making their debut that season were Over the Rockies, a ride in a tub in and out of dark tunnels, The Bug House, a shooting gallery, and the 'Kentucky Derby' game.

Ocean Park residents were proud of their new pier, and realized that they needed a convention center to accomodate thousands of visiting delegates. They approved $375,000 in bonds in the May election to build a new auditorium, bandstand, and auto park on the north side of the Pickering Pier. The bandstand plaza in front of the auditorium could entertain 10,000 people, and the auto park set on pilings behind the building could accomodate 500 autos.

Two hundred men worked diligently to finish the pier, buildings and attractions in time for the June 18, 1920 grand opening. It was a weekend of celebration in which all the rides operated at capacity throughout the day until midnight, and the dance hall was full of happy couples. Twenty five thousand people came on Saturday; 60,000 people on Sunday. Their fun filled day was capped with a 30 minute fireworks display each evening.

Stockholders were certainly pleased with business that summer. Pickering declared and paid one percent dividends on a monthly basis. In August he hired Barr's Illuminated Aerial Circus to entertain nightly. The plane had lights outlining it as it did tricks. Seventy five thousand people watched the show the first night.

Venice also had a successful summer. A crowd estimated at 125,000 visited Venice on Fourth of July

Aerial view of the Abbot Kinney Pier in December 1920, just two weeks before it was destroyed by fire.

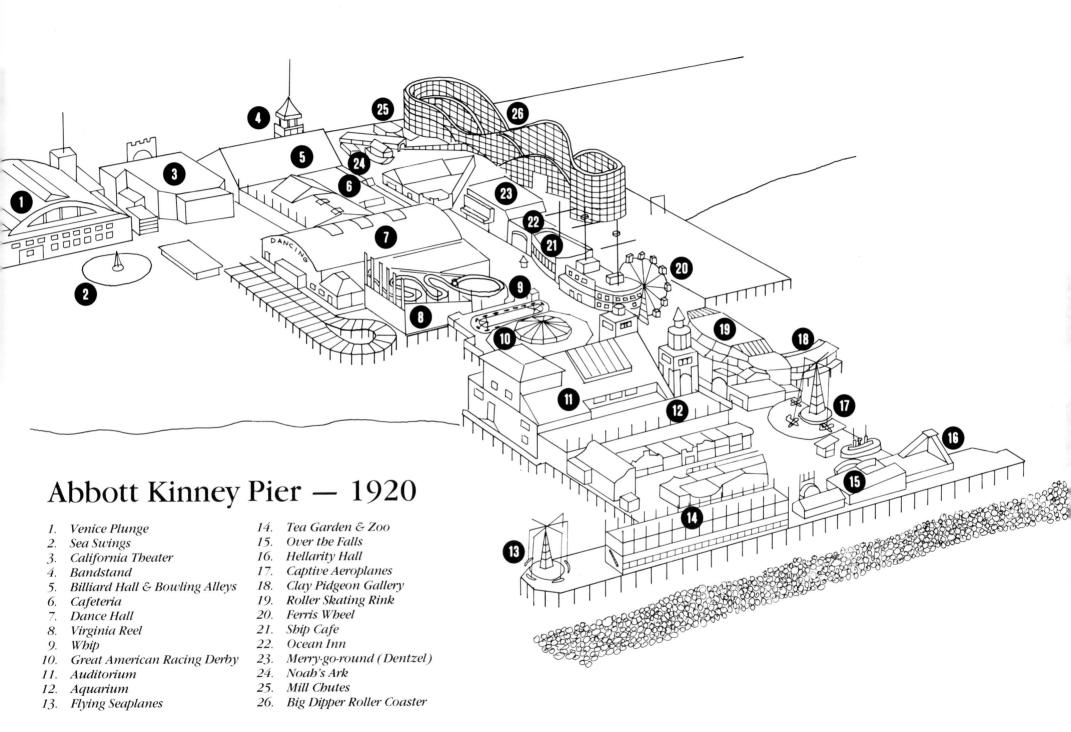

Abbott Kinney Pier — 1920

1. Venice Plunge
2. Sea Swings
3. California Theater
4. Bandstand
5. Billiard Hall & Bowling Alleys
6. Cafeteria
7. Dance Hall
8. Virginia Reel
9. Whip
10. Great American Racing Derby
11. Auditorium
12. Aquarium
13. Flying Seaplanes
14. Tea Garden & Zoo
15. Over the Falls
16. Hellarity Hall
17. Captive Aeroplanes
18. Clay Pidgeon Gallery
19. Roller Skating Rink
20. Ferris Wheel
21. Ship Cafe
22. Ocean Inn
23. Merry-go-round (Dentzel)
24. Noah's Ark
25. Mill Chutes
26. Big Dipper Roller Coaster

weekend. The city's local ordinance against fireworks was virtually unenforcible during the holiday. Children violating the law were so numerous that they defied the police, even ridiculed them. Everyone had fun, spent their money freely, and by the end of the holiday merchants had deposited $500,000 at the local banks.

There was nothing like a bit of competition to improve a ride. Frank Prior and Fred Church renewed their lease at the end of the summer for the Race Thru the Clouds racing coaster in anticipation of rebuilding it by the end of the year. They planned to tear down the entire ride and build a faster one with steeper dips and more thrills. The first drop would be nearly 90 feet, followed by a second drop of 80 feet. Improvements would cost them $50,000.

The newly incorporated Sunset Pier Company looked like they were finally going to do something with their leasehold on the Center Street Pier. In late September they announced that they were building a horseshoe pier that would extend out 500 feet, then make a 45 degree bend to connect with another pier to be built latter at Mildred Avenue. On the south side of the pier would be a replica of an Ocean Liner with all of the amusement features found on the big passenger steam ships. It would have a swimming plunge, bowling alleys, restaurant and cabaret. They were negotiating with C. W. Parker, builder of the Steeple Chase ride at Coney Island, to build a duplicate on their pier.

Abbot Kinney, whose health was failing, collapsed and became bedridden in late October. His condition worsened, and after only a few sporadic periods of conscious in the ensuing weeks he died on Thursday November 4, 1920 at 6:20 A.M. The "Doge" of Venice's death was not sudden. It was known for months to his staff and family that he was dying of lung cancer and Bright's Kidney disease. Meanwhile he discussed the transfer of power to his eldest son, 34 year old Thornton. When the end came at dawn that cool day in November, the businesses and amusements closed their doors in mourning, and all the flags in Venice were flown at half mast. Out of respect the pier remained closed Friday night.

Kinney was buried at Woodlawn Cemetery in Santa Monica beside his first wife Margaret who had died in 1911. His grave was covered with four truck loads of flowers as hundreds stood by during the ceremony. As a final tribute the Venice of America Band played 'My Roseary!, My Roseary!'.

Six weeks later disaster struck. It was on a cool night on December 20th at 9:30 P.M. People were huddled

St Marks Hotel at Windward Avenue and Ocean Front Walk; 1920.

around a gas heater in one of the upstairs loges of the dance pavilion on the Venice Pier. Suddenly the heater burst open, its flames leaped to the curtains and then to the roof timbers. There was no panic. The orchestra played an exit march as the dancers quickly left. Ten minutes later the roof collapsed throwing great masses of burning timbers to the floor. Arthur Ranse, a volunteer firefighter, was on the roof when it caved in. He was hurled into the seething furnace, but was rescued by some of the dancers and lay dying in a nearby hospital.

Flames spread quickly to the adjoining Virginia Reel, then to the Whip, Racing Derby and Auditorium. Firefighters on arrival dipped their hoses into the nearby lagoon and Venice Plunge. A score of people, mostly concessionaires, some who were attempting to save the seals at the Aquarium, were trapped at the end of the pier. One former lifeguard made three rescue trips in a row boat to the rock jetty, but his boat overturned on his return from the third trip. The few that remained sought safety in an open boat and by morning were still bobbing around at the outer edge of the breaker line.

By 10 P.M. the fire was conceded to be out of control. With the wind still blowing on-shore, warnings were sent to all merchants across Ocean Front Walk and along Windward. They hastily dragged the contents of their stores into the streets, and all hotels and apartment buildings were quickly evacuated.

Fireman used dynamite in a futile attempt to stop the fire at the outer boundaries of the pier. When this failed, Venice firemen, reinforced by fire companies from Santa Monica and Los Angeles, set up a mighty barrage of water to save the Ocean Front buildings. They concentrated on saving the California Theater and St. Marks Hotel. All seemed lost when suddenly the wind shifted and blew offshore at 11:30 P.M.

The next morning the pier was a smoldering ruin. One fireman had lost his life. The mammoth dance pavilion, Ship's Cafe, auditorium, aquarium, and all the amusement rides were gone. Only the newly built Big Dipper roller coaster and bandstand tower miraculously survived. Damages ran to a million dollars, with little of it insured. It was a bleak Christmas.

The city Trustees immediately set up a 'White Way' along Ocean Front Walk from the Plunge to the Center Street Pier as temporary quarters for concessionaires. The area was brilliantly illuminated with strings of lights. The Kinney Company converted the Plunge into a dance hall for the New Year's Eve Carnival, and Church-Prior succeeded into putting both of their

The Abbot Kinney Pier burned on December 20, 1920. The undamaged Captive Airplane ride at the end of the pier is in the background.

roller coasters into operation in time for the holiday. It was commendable that Venice's amusement people didn't lose heart, and instead of bewailing their misfortune, began planning a reopening.

Thornton Kinney, who had taken over his father's business, announced that the pier would be rebuilt by summer and would be even better. Despite the fact that the city couldn't afford to lose a season without its chief source of income, financing proved difficult. Two separate bond issues offered by the Kinney heirs were required to finance the rebuilding which took place that spring. It was money that could have been put to better use. The financially strapped Kinney Company, due to inheritance taxes and rising labor costs, found it increasingly difficult to keep the large crew of men needed to clear out the floatsam thrown into the canals by careless visitors.

During the same period Ed Dunnavant's Sunset Amusement Company was taking advantage of the Kinney Company's misfortune. They succeeded in issuing $700,000 in stock for their project, promoting it as the only pier currently under construction in Venice and with the Abbot Kinney pier burned, one without competition. Nearby land values tripled. A $2500 lot on the south beach was suddenly worth $7500.

Prior and Church, in charge of the reconstruction of the Venice Pier, began removing the burned out ruins in early February. Railcars of lumber arrived several weeks later in time for workers to begin pile driving. By April 15th the last of the pier pilings was in place and the decking extended two-thirds to the end. The rebuilt pier was 1200 feet long and 525 feet wide. It looked like they would make their May 28th target for the pier's opening when the workman went on strike. The gripe was that the out of town carpenters were paid less than the union men on the job. Fortunately, the strike was settled quickly.

The Kinney Company was building an enormous new dance hall. An oval shaped orchestra pit was placed in the center of a hardwood maple dance floor 180 feet wide by 210 feet deep. Balconies extending around the entire pavilion included banquet rooms and a private ballroom. The indirect lit interior was decorated in a Spanish motif, a suggestion of Moorish origin.

Many of the ride and concession operators on the old pier leased space on the new pier. The Howse Building on the northwest corner of the pier entrance would contain 18 billiard tables and fourteen bowling alleys. The new Ship Cafe, now facing the water perpendicular to the pier, would be built on a slightly larger scale, 160 feet long and 95 feet wide. Ellis purchased another

Prior and Church rebuilt the Race Thru the Clouds roller coaster with steeper and higher dips. They also constructed a much more ornate entrance at Trolley Way; 1921.

Aerial view of the rebuilt Venice Pier midway; 1923.

Ocean Front Walk looking north from Windward Avenue; 1921.

Dentzel Carousel and planned to install it in a 90 feet square building on the north side of the pier. The owners of Over the Falls, Noah's Ark, the Great American Racing Derby and the Captive Aeroplanes rides were planning to reopen with new and improved versions.

Prior and Church were also building a toboggan roller coaster adjacent to their Big Dipper coaster. Each of the bobsled shaped cars in the nine car trains would seat two passengers, one behind the other. The ride called 'Bobs', short for Bob Sleds, was the first coaster designed entirely by Fred Church. It was 60 feet high, had 2700 feet of track and had tight banked dropping turns. Trains went up the main hill, plunged down the big drop, around a bend, then up through a long tunnel almost in one fluid motion. His newly patented cars with three point suspension and a shorter wheel base enabled the cars to negotiate the sharper turns. Each of the articulated cars, except the first, had two wheels and were connected to each other by a ball and socket joint. Church's design philosophy differed markedly from Miller's, who never liked to design coasters with banked turns.

Beach Amusement Corporation was installing Dodge 'em and Gadabout rides in the same building. The electrically powered ride had a steel floor and overhead trolley. The double seat Dodge 'em cars were fully steerable, while the patrons in the single seat Gadabout cars lacked control and were always going in a direction they least expected. The fun was in safely smashing into other cars that were protected by large rubber bumpers.

The pier, risen from the ashes, staged a comeback on Memorial Day May 28, 1921. It wasn't the official opening; that would come later on July 4th, but the Dance Hall, Plunge and some of the rides on the unfinished pier were open for a curious public. It was estimated that the new pier cost the Kinney family some three million dollars.

The roar of the roller coaster and its screaming passengers near the pier's entrance immediately attracted one's attention. A sign over the entrance stated the obvious, "This is sure some wicked ride." A weight guesser on the midway offered people a chance to win an ornate plaster kewpie doll if he missed. He allowed a six pound margin of error. The salt water taffy store beyond had a twin armed mechanical contraption in the window that fascinated children. It pulled and tugged at the sugary candy as its arms went round until it became taffy. There were a dozen flavors of the sticky one cent candy available. The sound of carnival music

beckoned one on. It came from the carousel's mechanical pipe organ. Young children filled the ride as their parents stood watching from the side. Those riding on the outside animals stretched to grab the brass ring as the carrousel went round and round.

Some lease space near the end of the pier was still available. One imaginative entrepreneur planned to build a 92 foot high tower with 1000 square feet of ground space. It would contain a merry-go-round on the bottom which would rise as it turned until it was 60 feet high. Riders would find themselves on an entirely new story. Stairs would lead to a dance pavilion with an observation balcony and roof garden 72 feet above ground. People would have a choice of descending down a bamboo slide or ride the elevator. Although a ride like this existed in the midwest, it was one of many rides that just never got built in Venice.

Venice promoters staged a double celebration that Fourth of July as both the Venice Pier and the Sunset Pier officially opened. Entertainers were everywhere; comedy teams along Ocean Front Walk, 'yama yama' girls serpentine dancing on the pier, and bands playing at various locations. One hundred seventy five thousand visitors had a choice of either going to the beach and watching the aerial stunt show performed by Bill Delay and R. A. Boyd, or visiting one of the new piers to try out dozens of new attractions. The Lew Lewis Orchestra was performing at the Venice Dance Hall, and the 26 member 'Baby Doll Dance Revue' entertained crowds at the nearby Sunset Ballroom.

Prior's new Great American Racing Derby was even larger than his previous ride. Its 56 horses each had double saddles to accomodate couples or a parent and child. Raymond's 18 tub Whirl-i-gig ride was spinning patrons until they were dizzy, while the Captive Aeroplanes, Zig Zag, Dodge' em, Bob's and Big Dipper Coasters were accomodating long lines of customers throughout the day and evening.

Mechanical games of skill were ever popular with the crowds. Competitors could try their skill at the 'Cat Rack' booth by knocking kittens off a fence, or race sailboats at the 'Yacht Race' booth by blowing air at scale model boats set in three inch deep channels. Then there was the 'Kentucky Derby' game where competitors would race miniature horses activated by tossing balls accurately into a hole, and other games like 'Dart the Dart', 'Blow Ball Race' and 'Race in the Jungle'. By the time the weekend ended, amusement owners deposited $800,000 in the banks.

Ocean Park got a big boost in September when

Charles Lick, Austin McFadden and George Leihy invested $250,000 in the construction of a new pier behind the Dome Dance Pavilion. The proposed Lick Pier at the foot of Navy Street adjoining the south side of the Pickering Pier was almost entirely within Venice's boundary.

The 800 foot long, 225 foot wide pier was to have a roller coaster, dance hall, 40 car Dodge 'em, Caterpillar, Captive Aeroplanes and Limit rides. McFadden, who was in charge of construction, hired John A. Miller to design his roller coaster. Plans were for the longest and steepest pier roller coaster in the Bay area. Each of its dips would be double instead of single; down 75 feet, up 60 feet, down 58 feet. They called the 600 foot long coaster the 'Zip' when it opened in time for Easter in 1922.

Lick's new 22,000 square foot Bon Ton Ballroom featured an oval-shaped dance floor for better acoustics. The hall was large enough to be split into two separate ballrooms with different orchestras. Major Baisden's twelve piece orchestra was the first to entertain dancers when it opened. The old Dome Dance Hall was converted into a theater, and a Casino was under construction across from it on Ocean Front Walk just north of Navy Street. It too would have a dance hall and shops, with billiards and bowling in the basement.

Pickering made only a few changes to his pier that spring. He added the Double Whirl, Dodge 'em, and the Witching Waves rides to round out the amusements. The latter ride had been a big hit at Luna Park in Coney Island. People rode a boat shaped car around an oval track, propelled by the down grade of a moving mechanical wave. Bell cranks and huge connecting rods imparted the wave motion to the ride's flexible metal flooring.

The Double Whirl had cars set on a figure eight track with a slight incline where the two circular sections crossed. The cars were pushed by radial arms, rotating around the two fixed hubs. When the cars approached each other at the top and collision appeared inevitable, each car would glide into the other circle.

Leroy Raymond was the only one to add anything to Kinney's Pier that summer. His new and improved Noah's Ark attraction, a large biblical replica that rocked, was finally finished. Funseekers entered the ark across a wooden walkway at the top and worked their way to the exit at the bottom. Inside was a maze of passages in which disoriented patrons wandered past stalls featuring pairs of animals that Noah saved from the flood. It was a good rendition of one of mankind's

Sunset Pier and Ballroom looking through the Big Dipper roller coaster on the Venice Pier; 1923.

favorite Biblical story. The lower portion, which was stationary, had rippling floors and various fun house stunts like snakes and spiders that jumped out and a revolving barrel.

The early 20's was an exuberant era in which people sought excitement, and Venice and its newly rebuilt pier fit the bill. Hollywood film stars like Mary Pickford, Douglas Fairbanks, Fatty Arbuckle, and Charles Chaplin, as well as some underworld figures, kept summer homes along the canals or on the beach front. It was an atmosphere in which wild parties and sensational news stories thrived.

It was during the spring of 1922 that stories of a municipal scandal began to circulate among the citizenry. On May 3, 1922, the Venice Vanguard confirmed the rumors that James T. Peasgood Jr., City Treasurer since 1914, was overdue on a fishing vacation to Oxnard, California. Over $23,000 in city funds were reported missing.

There had been rumors, just the year before, that Venice's municipal government was on the verge of bankruptcy. When the Los Angeles Grand Jury made inquiries, the mayor resigned. It was true that treasurer Peasgood had a habit of depositing city funds in certain banks without collecting interest, but the charges had been dismissed.

When city Trustees ordered an independent audit in April 1922, Peasgood panicked. He told his wife that he was going fishing, but fled to Toledo, Ohio via San Francisco and Chicago. Trustees opened his safety deposit box and found $28,500 in securities.

Weeks later Peasgood, deciding to give himself up, called his wife from Ventura, California. When authorities picked him up on May 17th, he confessed to having embezzled since 1918, to supplement his $135/month salary and pay his gambling losses. An independent auditor set the shortage at $19,000. That winter Peasgood was sentenced to San Quentin Prison for one to ten years. Although the insurance company that bonded Peasgood paid the city $15,000, the whole affair caused a lack of confidence in the city officials.

Almost at the same time the Peasgood story broke, city Trustees became embarrassed by their decision to lease the bankrupt Sunset Pier to Henry Singer for $50,000. They were influenced by personal testimonials made by leading citizens concerning his good character and business acumen. Three days later Singer was held in a psychiatric ward of the county hospital for assaulting Marco Mellman, a banker at Merchant's National Bank in Los Angeles, when he was refused a loan.

Sunset Ballroom on the Sunset Pier at Center Street (North Venice Boulevard); 1922. (above)

Noah's Ark fun house on the Venice Pier; 1924. (below)

Investigation revealed that Singer's only asset was his ability to get others to place their confidence in him.

Despite the scandals there were hopeful signs and the outlook of the community became more positive. Business conditions were improving. The city, benefiting from increased real estate sales and new building starts, reduced the property tax rate. But still other serious problems continued to haunt the city.

The automobile age produced problems never considered when Venice was planned. By the 1920's, as more and more residents and visitors travelled by car, Venice suffered from inadequate parking and traffic congestion. The city had no major thoroughfare except Lincoln Boulevard, and that road didn't pass through the central portion of Venice. Trolleyway would have made an excellent north-south artery if widened and paved, but the Pacific Electric resisted efforts to have its right of way transformed into a highway. The canals, which were intended for transportation as well as aesthetic values, never had the utility their designers intended.

The lack of an internal transportation network or an overall master plan, coupled with an irregular and elongated-shaped city, fostered the growth of widely separated government, business and commercial districts. As the Windward business district proved to be too small to accomodate the city's rapid growth, other business centers developed including the Ocean Park Pier business district centering around Marine Street, the area next to city hall where Shell Avenue met the Short Line Track and an area near the Center Street Pier. The existence of these centers and the lack of any central hub created political factionalism that weakened and often paralyzed Venice's municipal government.

There were other problems such as an undependable supply of fresh water delivered by three water companies, a city owned incinerator whose volume of garbage had outgrown capacity and an inadequate municipally owned sewer system that had been designed in 1912 for 3000 people. The sewer system was so badly overloaded that at times the State Board of Health quarantined much of the ocean and beach on both sides of the outfall at the Center Street Pier. A new treatment plant had been designed, but voters did not approve the sale of bonds in the April 11, 1922 election.

By the fall of 1922 the 750 member Chamber of Commerce resolved to act. Although there was much talk of consolidation with Santa Monica, they were firmly committed to retaining Venice's civic identity. Instead, they favored a change to a city manager form of government.

Interior of the Venice Dance Hall.

Ocean Front Walk looking north from the Venice Plunge tower; 1922.

Lick Pier showing Bon Ton Ballroom and Zip roller coaster; 1922. (above)

Ocean Park Bathhouse and beach; 1924. (left)

The Trustees voted to submit the new charter to the people in the February 20, 1923 election. A city manager charter would keep the city's business out of politics. Practically every municipal organization favored the ballot measure. But before the election occurred, a petition urging consolidation with Santa Monica was able to secure sufficient signatures to have the question added to the ballot. Although 100 citizens alleged that their signatures were forged, the Trustees nonetheless accepted it. Then the Trustees, less than a month before the election, further befuddled the electorate by placing on the ballot a series of bond issues totaling $1,600,000.

All ballot measures were defeated. The public was clearly dissatisfied, but each faction had opposed one another's solutions.

Petitions for annexation to Los Angeles began to circulate that spring. People were willing to sign because conditions were deteriorating rapidly and they began to look elsewhere to solve their governmental problems. When 2000 signatures were obtained and presented to the Board of Trustees, they had no choice by law but to authorize an election for July 10, 1923.

The Trustees, attempting to squash annexationists' selling points and also save their political skins, voted to

proceed with various street improvements, including the paving of Trolleyway. In April, plans were announced by Ben Brodsky, a Venice businessman, to merge the three existing water companies and expand them. The next month city health officers announced that the ban of swimming on the south beach was being lifted because the purifying plant had been installed at the Venice sewer outfall which lay beneath the Sunset Pier. And on June 4th, in a last ditch effort to forestall annexation, the Trustees voted to create the position of city manager and hire someone by July.

The advocates of annexation continued to hammer away at the factionalism that had paralyzed the city in the past. One thousand more voters went to the polls than had voted in February. Although some part-time citizens may have been among the 3,352 voters, annexation lost by 346 votes; 1849 to 1503. A heavy turnout by Windward and the canal district voters saved the city.

A new round of friendly pier competition was renewed that season. When Prior and Church signed a lease at the Pickering Pier for a new roller coaster between Pier Ave and the Ocean Park Auditorium (the site of the Blarney Racer), the Kinney Company announced plans for $500,000 in new attractions and improvements. Foremost was a new $200,000 Fun House, a half acre structure which would be along the lines of the fun place at Steeplechase Park in Coney Island. It would contain 25 different types of rides, slides and freak amusements. The lobby would be like a high class theater.

When the Fun House opened several months later, it became one of the most beloved attractions on the Venice Pier. For a mere nickle children would spend hours exploring its vast interior. There was a tall metal slide and a smaller bamboo slide six lanes wide that would end in a rotating barrel. Two large spinning Society Wheels, turntables that dared children and adults to hang on until last while everyone else was flung off to the edges, stood near the center. There were stacks of barrels that rocked and looked like they would fall and crush some unlucky person, and a Mystery Room where one tried to find their way out. One could stand around and watch the hidden airjets, controlled by a man below, try to blow the girl's skirts above their waists, or ride a small roller coaster up in the rafters. It encircled the entire structure and made its deepest dip at the front between the entrance and exit doors.

Work was begun on the mammoth $175,000 Flying Circus aerial ride, a locally designed attraction by John Metzer's engineering firm. Plans called for six large, 2200 pound, eight passenger airplanes to load at a point west of the ballroom, then proceed on track in a tunnel to the main tower. As the cars approached the main tower, a cable mechanism would lift them to simulate the take off of an airplane. Attached to huge rotating metal arms, the planes would climb in a widening arc until they were 64 feet off the ground and flying in a circle 242 feet in diameter. An operator located in a tower opposite the ride could, using twelve controls, make the planes go into a tailspin or take a nosedive before straightening out. The planes would travel two and one half miles at 50 MPH before landing. Due to difficult engineering problems work on the ride proceeded at a snails pace, and would take an additional two years to build.

H. W. McGeary, owner of the One-Eyed Circus at the end of the pier, moved and remodeled it to make way for the new roller coaster. Some Kick roller coaster, yet another Miller design was to cost $60,000. McGeary was also constructing a Glass House, a mirror maze type attraction. Others were installing a Pig Slide, Automatic Baseball Pitcher, Caterpillar ride, Spark Plug and Deep Sea Diving concessions. And the owner of the Captive Aeroplanes was installing several children's rides near the end of the pier. Prior lowered the price of the Bobs, Big Dipper, Race Thru the Clouds and Racing Derby rides to ten cents because Venice was becoming known as a 'gyp town'.

The Pickering Pier's big Whip ride arrived from San Francisco and was placed next to to Merry-go-round where the Frolic once stood. The Captive Airplanes was moved to a new location and a Caterpillar ride was added to the main midway.

The new Giant Dipper roller coaster opened in time for Memorial Day. The 85 foot high, 3300 foot long ride featuring tight banked dropping turns in true twister fashion and was an immediate success. It did more business than any other west coast roller coaster to date, and Prior paid stockholders monthly dividends totalling 25 percent in its first four months of operation.

The coaster was a 'Bobs' design, a twister roller coaster set in a figure eight pattern. When the 22 passenger train plunged down the first drop at a 55 degree angle, it was practically a free falling body that was calculated to leave its passenger's stomach's behind as they rose out of their seats and hung on with tightly clenched fists to the restraining bar. It then zoomed up another hill, banked and curved at the top, then down a series of dips and crossed through the lift hill structure. The two minute ride up and down a dozen additional hills was rough and subjected passengers to a continous series of accelerations, decelerations, jolts and bounces that gave everyone their money's worth of thrills.

Although the Giant Dipper was the last roller coaster Prior and Church designed for the Venice / Ocean Park area, their designs continued to evolve during the 'Golden Era' of roller coasters through the late 1920's. They formed a loose partnership with Harry Traver, who often acted as a regional sales rep in the east. They designed them and Traver Engineering built most of them. These included the following Bob designs; Chicago's Riverview Park Bobs (1924), Santa Monica's Whirlwind Dipper (1924), Revere Beach Cyclone (1925), Savin Rock's Thunderbolt (1925), San Diego's Belmont Park Earthquake (1925), Coney Island's Tornado (1926), Rye Playland's Bobs/Airplane (1928) and Long Beach's Cyclone Racer (1930). Their roller coasters were customized with different track layouts and sizes for each park. They were all bigger and more terrifying than the small Bobs on the Venice Pier. The last two coasters were designed by Fred Church after his partnership with Prior ended.

Overt gambling had always been an integral part of Venice's fun zone. Razzle dazzle and layout games, where spinning wheels determined the prizewinners, proliferated along the boardwalk and piers. Their legality was questionable. Arrests were made periodically by crusading district attorneys and local police.

Larger scale gambling was also the de-rigueur. Whether the gaming took place in private dining rooms at the Ship Cafe or in small casinos in the basements of various hotels and restaurants, if one were looking for a place to lose their money it was easily found.

In September 1923 the police raided a gambling club that occupied the quarters of the Submarine Garden, once a high class cafe beneath the old Dome Pier. They found a maze of tunnels, cards and $150 on the tables then arrested fifteen alleged gamblers.

The place was very difficult to raid. It looked like a pool room, but the back of the room led to a long tunnel with branches leading every which way. Exotic futuristic paintings, water stained and covered with cobwebs, decorated the walls, and secret doors opened behind angles in the tunnel. Sand, covering the tunnel floor, concealed secret buttons which operated a system of buzzers and colored lights in the main rooms of the labyrinth. The system of tunnels was so involved that it took two hours to find the fifteen arrested, and at least that many more were believed to have escaped. As soon as Lick found out about it, he closed the club.

During the years that Prohibition was in effect, Canadian liquor was smuggled into Venice from offshore rumrunners by high-powered motorboats that docked beneath the pier in the dead of night. Mobster Tony Cornero ran the operation. Kinney's underground utility tunnels along the alleys on either side of Windward Avenue proved handy to the smugglers who delivered to 'speakeasy' bars in the basements of the business district. There were a few newspaper accounts of police engaging in shootouts with rumrunners along the beach near the Ocean Park Pier.

It was an open secret that there were 'speakeasys' in the basements of the Antler Hotel on the lagoon and beneath Menotti's Grocery store and other businesses on Windward. A man-lift in the back alley behind the store carried those who gave the right password from the hide-away street level door to the sinful caverns below. Considering the amount of police corruption in those days, it isn't surprising that there were rarely any raids and arrests at these places. 'Dry agents', however, did crack down and raid various houses in the area, especially along the sparsely populated Venice peninsula, where they confiscated huge caches of liquor.

The slow winter months were often the best time to

Ocean Front Walk at the Pickering / Lick Piers; 1923

plan or rebuild new amusements. Church-Prior, after agreeing to tear down their Race Thru the Clouds coaster to make way for a new civic center, decided to replace the Big Dipper coaster on the pier with their newer Giant Dipper model. Although the old coaster was built in 1919 and was considered the last word in coaster design when it was built, the Venice Pier needed a new ride that would compete with the coaster in Ocean Park. It took 90 days to build the $100,000 ride, a virtual duplicate although a slightly smaller version of the one installed the previous spring in Ocean Park.

Another disastrous fire occurred in early 1924. This time both the Pickering and Lick piers in Ocean Park were totally consumed in an early morning blaze on January 6th. The fire was believed to have started at 9:30 A.M. in the Ritz Cafe kitchen, but it didn't explain how the fire spread so rapidly. Some thought that rubbish was set ablaze beneath the pier near the restaurant.

When fireman first arrived it seemed like the Municipal Auditorium was doomed. Firetrucks laid hoses, but before the water could be turned on, flames burst up from underneath and the entire walk was ablaze and the hoses burned. Another firetruck broke and the water stopped.

The wind blowing offshore towards the southwest rose to its height and all of Ocean Park was threatened. Rumors that 'they were going to dynamite' scattered the huge crowd who lined up on every street to watch. They became panic stricken. Many of the concessionaires who became trapped on the pier dove into the cold water.

Ten fire companies fought the blaze. The shift of the wind by several points at 11 A.M. had firemen worried. Had it blown parallel to the beach, it would have devastated the entire business district. Luckily the Dome Theater's concrete structure at the northeast corner of the pier contained the fire and prevented it from leaping across Ocean Front Walk. By 11:45 A.M. firemen had the fire under control, and not one building east of Ocean Front Walk had burned.

The losses were enormous, $2,000,000, with only $100,000 of the loss insured. Both the Rosemary and Dome Theaters were destroyed, the latter's loss alone was set at $500,000. All of the pier's rides and concessions were completely destroyed, with the exception of the sea end section of the Giant Dipper coaster. Frank Prior thought he could rebuild it because the ride's most difficult section was intact. They and everyone else would have to await new owners.

Crowd watches the Ocean Park pier and Dome Theater burn. (above)

Remains of the Ocean Park Pier include the west end of the Giant Dipper.

SPENCE
Air Photos

Ocean Park Pier burned Sunday morning January 6, 1924. The entire pier was destroyed. Aerial view of the still smoldering pilings was taken that afternoon.

CHAPTER 5

Annexation & Ruin (1924-1929)

The Venice Investment Company and West Coast Theaters acquired Pickering's beach holdings for $2,000,000 just two weeks after the fire. The sale was a windfall for Pickering, who took a terrible loss and would have had difficulty financing a new concrete and fireproof pier that Santa Monica would have insisted upon. The new owners got a 50 year lease on the beach property, or at least they thought they did.

When they applied for a building permit in mid February, city officials in Santa Monica informed them that they wouldn't grant a permit but would instead lease the sand which they claimed the city owned. Santa Monica officials intended to advertise for bids for a pier franchise on their property. The stunned new owners filed for an injunction to stop the bidding.

The auction took place at City Hall on March 18, 1924. The Venice Investment Company, intent on regaining control of the pier property, out bid several other companies. Their winning bid was $2000 / month. The next day they announced plans to rebuild the pier at a cost of $3,000,000 and begin work one week later. Other than clearing the site, little was accomplished that spring. Work would begin in earnest on the pier in the fall.

Owners of both the Dome and Rosemary theaters on Ocean Front Walk put higher priority on reopening than the Venice Investment Company did. The Rosemary Theater began operating immediately in temporary quarters on the promenade at Kinney Street. The new 1600 seat Dome Theater, rebuilt in only 23 days, opened May 30th at the proposed entrance to the pier. The original interior had a Spanish design, but the following spring they redecorated it with an Egyptian motif to match the theme of the new dance hall. They also added a $65,000 organ.

Lick, whose pier resided across the Venice boundary line, was able to begin reconstruction almost immediately after the fire. Work on his pier progressed rapidly, and by May 14th the Bon Ton Ballroom was ready for paying customers. The interior of the enlarged ballroom was decorated in a modified Louis XV motif. Caryle Stevenson and his orchestra entertained nightly and all day on weekends.

Lick's new pier was basically the same layout as his old pier; the Bon Ton Ballroom, Dodge 'em ride and a

View of Ocean Front Walk looking north at the rebuild Ocean Park Pier; 1925.

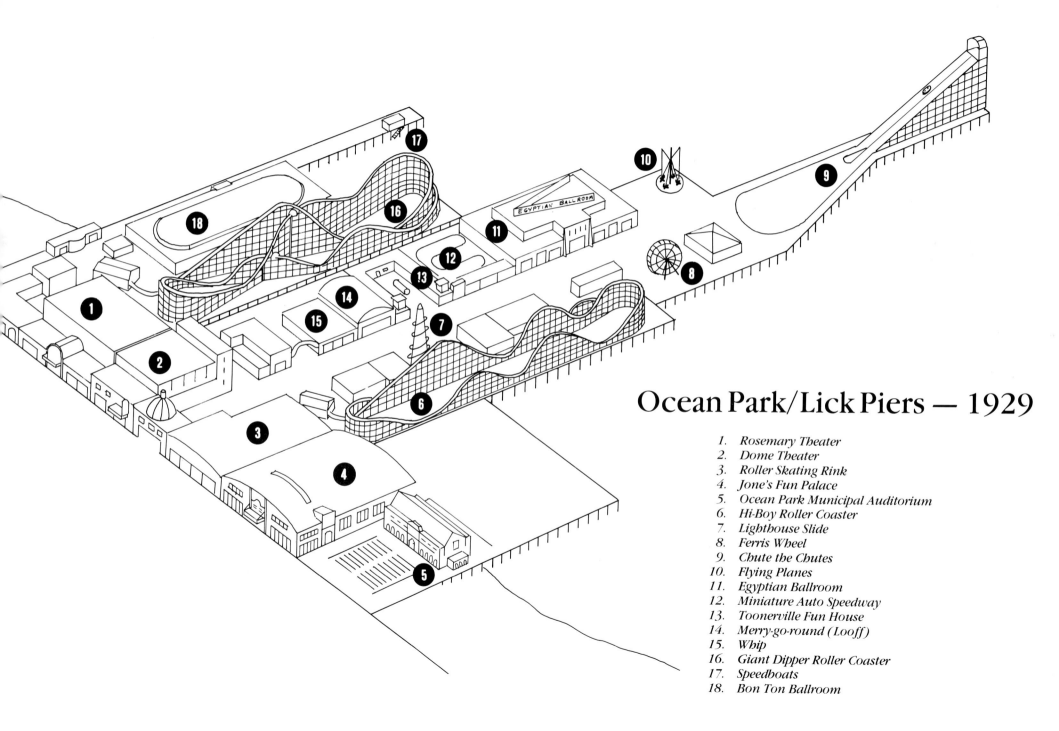

Ocean Park/Lick Piers — 1929

1. Rosemary Theater
2. Dome Theater
3. Roller Skating Rink
4. Jone's Fun Palace
5. Ocean Park Municipal Auditorium
6. Hi-Boy Roller Coaster
7. Lighthouse Slide
8. Ferris Wheel
9. Chute the Chutes
10. Flying Planes
11. Egyptian Ballroom
12. Miniature Auto Speedway
13. Toonerville Fun House
14. Merry-go-round (Looff)
15. Whip
16. Giant Dipper Roller Coaster
17. Speedboats
18. Bon Ton Ballroom

View of the beach and south side of the rebuilt Lick Pier in Ocean Park; 1926.

few concessions along the south side of the pier, with space for a roller coaster behind. Lick needed a new roller coaster for the summer so he contracted Prior and Church to rebuild their famous Giant Dipper coaster on the site formally occupied by the Zip. The 85 feet high ride opened July 4, 1924.

The 1924 spring election brought to power an administration that seemed bent on self-destruction. The Civic Betterment League slate, C. Gordon Parkhurst, H.L. Anderman and Thomas Thurlow, gained control of the Board of Trustees and had no ties to the Kinney Company. They were committed to local government only if public confidence could be restored to enable financing of a comprehensive series of civic improvements. However, one of their ideas of improving Venice in the name of progress was to build more roads. That meant paving the Pacific Electric's right of way on Trolley Way and filling in the canals. The Kinney family, discarding sentiment, cooperated by deeding all of the canals north of Venice Boulevard to the city.

The canal property owners were in an uproar. A public hearing to decide the fate of the canals, which had been scheduled before the Trustees voted, was declared a sham when public officials didn't show. At this point the canals owners, who had no recourse, went to court in an effort to prevent the transformation of the waterways into roadways. They argued that the project would result in a special assessment to their property and they would would lose the parklike character of their district. The judge granted them a temporary injunction on August 6, 1924.

That same week the Sunset Pier was sold to the Electric Pier and Amusement Company. The $75,000 price included the pier's Sunset Ballroom. The new owners, whose company was capitalized at $1.5 million, had ambitious plans. They planned to build a new pier with a surface area of 20.5 acres, about six acres larger than Luna Park in Coney Island.

The pier's center piece would be the greatest outdoor swimming pool in the world. The 600 x 300 foot steel tank would feature a huge wave making machine that could generate waves 3 ½ feet high. In the center of the 18 inch to 9 feet deep pool would be an enormous electric fountain. The pool would be surrounded by 75 feet of sand beach.

The pier would accomodate 50,000 to 75,000 people who would each be charged ten cents admission. There would be a huge open air theater for 20,000 people on the sea end along with two aerial rides. The rides in the extensive amusement zone on either side of the swim-

Lighthouse Slide and midway looking east on the Ocean Park Pier.

Egyptian Ballroom on the Ocean Park Pier; 1925.

Entrance to the Hi-Boy roller coaster on the Ocean Park Pier.

ming pool would have the best attractions and rides available. The owners expected that work would begin at the first of the year and that they would open June 15, 1925.

The Coal Mine ride opened in September on the Venice Pier across from Some Kick roller coaster. The exterior looked like a mine shaft entrance in a rocky hillside and a powder house stood nearby. Burros pulled two passenger carts through a 550 foot long tunnel. The five minute ride was meant to be an educational experience in coal mining techniques.

By late November the Flying Circus ride on the pier was nearing completion. Workers were breaking in the bearings by slowly turning the massive 65 foot high steel turret. They had been working on it for nearly two and one half years, ever since they first poured the concrete foundations in May 1922.

Nearby in Ocean Park 200 men began working on the 960 foot long, 275 foot wide concrete pier. Work was progressing steadily and the owners expected it to open for Easter.

The Kinney Company meanwhile began having trouble with the new Board of Trustees. They passed an ordinance prohibiting miniature railroads from the city streets and gave the company a thirty day notice to quit. The Washington Street merchants, upon whose street the train ran, opposed the train's operation. Kinney, who operated the railroad as a unique means of advertising on weekends, shut the unprofitable operation down on Feb 13, 1925 and laid off four employees. The

Toonerville Fun House on the Ocean Park Pier; 1929.

railroad's rolling stock was eventually sold to a Denver businessman who moved it to Spokane, Washington.

A 98 foot high Dragon Bamboo Slide was erected in May on the Venice Pier. Customers climbed to the top of the cone-shaped tower, then slid down the spiral bamboo ramp on a straw mat. It was a thrilling ride for many, but one that would have more than its share of accidents as the slide aged. Bamboo splinters would often painfully impale people's rear ends as they slid down.

The Flying Circus, despite Meltzer's death in an automobile crash in April, opened in June. The ride was an engineering marvel, one so thrilling and realistic that the 48 passengers, eight each in six planes, thought they were actually flying. After the cars, circling the base on tracks, were attached to the six great rotating vertical arms, the arms were released two at a time to soar outwards. A device out at the end of each arm oscillated the cars, and powerful compressed air engines housed in the arms interrupted the plane's lift. This, combined with the plane's rising and falling as the speed was regulated, caused them to twist into spins and spirals as they circled the huge towers. The two minute ride was choreographed and the names of the manuevers posted each day.

The Egyptian Ballroom on June 27, 1925 was the first to open on the new Ocean Park Pier. The owners made a point of emphasizing the word 'fireproof' in all their advertising. They built the structure entirely of reinforced concrete and steel. The pier, too, was fireproofed with a concrete deck. Eight fire hydrants were connected to a 200,000 gallon tank on the roof of the Dome Theater.

The ballroom's interior was a replica in miniature of the temple of Rameses III, King of Egypt. Carvings on the wall painted in soft Egyptian colors depicted the likenesses of all the kings of the ancient kingdom on the Nile, and sketches depicted its historic highlights. There were scenes of Cleopatra and the death of Karasan, soul god of the Nile. Dance music was provided by Dave Snell's orchestra.

Jone's Fun Palace on Ocean Front Walk on the north side of the pier opened several days later. The large fun house style structure contained slides, rotating barrels, a miniature coaster, various kiddie rides and a large ornate Parker carousel. It was a large machine on a 48 foot diameter platform with 45 horses set three abreast. It also had two chariots and one row of very small horses.

The pier celebrated its grand opening with a ten day

A Parker carousel was located in Jone's Fun Palace building on the Ocean Park Pier until it was moved to the Venice Pier in 1929.

101

festival beginning on Saturday August 29, 1925. One hundred thousand people visited the pier on opening day and watched entertainers like Jake Cox make a fire dive into a tank of water. There were numerous new rides and attractions to suit people of all ages including the 75 foot tall Hi-Boy roller coaster, (another Miller design), an Aerial Swing, Speedboats, Flying Planes, the Rosemary Theater and a bowling and billiards center. The Lighthouse Slide towered 150 feet above the bay and almost beneath it was the Miniature Auto Speedway where pint-sized autos raced through tunnels and over hills.

Toonerville, the new fun house, looked from the midway like a village of dilapidated, possibly haunted shacks. Inside among its mostly dark winding passages were slides, rotating barrels and creepy things that scared you in the dark.

A Looff carousel was installed inside the Merry-go-round building. The three abreast menagerie style machine was an old model built in 1916. It had beautifully craved giraffes, rabbits, ostrichs, lions and stags among its rows of fancy white prancing horses.

Venice continued to become more and more politically impossible to govern. When a series of bond initiatives for public improvements totalling $1,185,000 failed to pass in the August 14, 1925 election, the Trustees called a special annexation election for October 2, 1925. Trustees Brown, Anderman, Reynolds and Parkhurst were initially for it. Anderman later changed sides and Thurlow was in Maine on family business.

Annexationists and anti-annexationists fought a bitter campaign. Signs in windows proclaimed, "Annexation Means Slavery" and "Annexation at Any Price." The "anti" group claimed that annexation would bring to Venetians "nothing but higher taxes, bossy interference with their affairs, slavery, bankruptcy and misery." It would be taxation without representation. The "pro" forces claimed that it would provide better police force, " and generally drag dear, blessed Venice out of the gutter."

Both sides threw counter charges at each other. Those who were "anti" pointed out what happened to other cities that had consolidated with Los Angeles. Their opponents charged that the amusement businesses were only concerned that Los Angeles' stiff "Blue Laws", which contained anti-gambling statutes and also banned Sunday and all night dancing, could close one-third of the piers. Ward McFadden, whose Ship Cafe was often the center of anti-annexation activities, was

Aerial view of the Ocean Park Pier and Santa Monica Bay. The small Bristol Pier, and larger Santa Monica Pier are further north, 1929.

View down the midway of the Ocean Park Pier shows the Lighthouse Slide and the Hi-Boy roller coaster on the right, 1927.

threatened with closure by the Venice Chief of Police.

Many influential citizens including Trustee H.L. Anderman and former mayor Dana Burke as well as the Venice Vanguard newspaper favored consolidation with Santa Monica as the more viable alternative. Three thousand people signed a petition to place it on the ballot if annexation lost. Even Thornton Kinney put up a $10,000 bond guaranteeing that if annexation failed that he would support merging with Santa Monica.

Out-of-towners temporarily moved into town, joined the right clubs and talked of nothing but annexation. Perhaps the residents listened, or perhaps they were willing to vote for any alternative to Venice's inept government. Annexation won 3130 to 2215.

Los Angeles officials, thrilled that at last they had added a beach district to their rapidly growing city, stated that they would proceed with the Venice's Trolley Way paving projects and fill in the canals once a decision was reached in Superior Court. Some Venice residents wanted to file an injunction to block annexation on the grounds that the two cities were not contiguous. However, no action was taken and Venice became part of Los Angeles as scheduled on November 25, 1925.

Venice's amusement zone was affected immediately by Los Angeles' Blue Laws. The Sunday dancing ban and anti-gambling statutes went in effect and pier business consequently suffered. The effect was most pronounced in the Ocean Park area. Huge Sunday crowds thronged the Ocean Park Pier, while few patrons wandered over to Venice's Lick Pier side where the Bon Ton Ballroom and other game concessions were closed. After two danceless Sundays amusement owners decided to campaign for a special amusement zone.

Prior and Church announced shortly after the election that they intended to build a $1.5 million fun zone at the foot of Leona Street (Washington Street) to be called Washington Pier. The 1200 foot long pier would have parking for 1500 automobiles. Attractions would include a bathing pool the size of the Plunge, a ballroom the size of the Bon Ton, a Giant Dipper coaster and a new Racing Bobs. It would be like the old Race Thru the Clouds roller coaster but instead of the cars running side by side, they would duck under one another and even lose sight of each other at times. But work on the proposed pier was held up because the City of Los Angeles intended to acquire all beach frontage including the leases.

Venice residents became concerned when Gordon Whiteall, Director of the Los Angeles City Regional

The Chute the Chutes ride was built on the end of the Ocean Park Pier in 1929. Sometimes it was used by dare devils to perform thrilling stunts as this woman did strapped to a rolling wheel. She planned to hit the pool at the bottom of the chute at high speed and survive.

Planning Commission, declared that it would be criminal if the city allowed another bit of her newly acquired strand to become cluttered up with "hurdy gurdy piers and other obstructions which will mar the gorgeous vista of nature's handiwork." He even suggested that the present piers be pushed back onto the mainland. Several days later apologetic officials clarified his statements and said the present piers would be left alone, but no new ones would be recommended.

Petitions circulated around Venice in January for an ordinance establishing a special amusement zone. By the end of the month 10,442 valid signers were certified among the 22,000 signatures collected. It was more than enough to compel the City Council to adopt the initiative ordinance attached to the petition.

At first they scheduled a a special election for April 30, 1926, but latter called it off when they feared that another measure on the ballot calling for pay increases for police and fireman might pass. The Council instead voted for Sunday dancing, at least temporarily. Two weeks later Mayor Cryer vetoed the Venice Amusement Zone Ordinance and rescheduled the April 30th election.

There was a big debate over the Sunday Blue Law measure. Its opponents were mostly churches aligned with ultra-conservatives. The Venice Chamber of Commerce countered that the blue laws drive business out of Venice into the unrestricted amusement zones in Santa Monica. It was definitely affecting business as 24 places went out of business and one-third of Edison's meters were idle in the amusement zone. They pointed out that Sunday was the only day a working person in Southern California could get away for pleasure.

The majority voted for the special amusement zone with all night Sunday dancing; 112,305 for it, 77,832 against it. The Venice vote was more than three to one in favor and Venice dance halls reopened for Sunday business May 16th.

The Venice Ballroom was once again crowded with Sunday dancers. Ben Pollack and his Californians occupied the ballroom bandstand. Customers, who bought forty dance tickets for a dollar, danced the charleston, fox trot, waltz and pivoting, a dance where the couple turned continously as they moved rapidly about the dance floor.

Attendents walked the floor and enforced the law against dancing 'cheek to cheek' by tapping the offending couple on the shoulder and instructing them to move apart. At the end of each five minute dance, attendents used a big long rope to herd the couples off

Venice Beach looking north from the Venice Pier was packed solid with bathers and their beach umbrellas every Sunday; 1926.

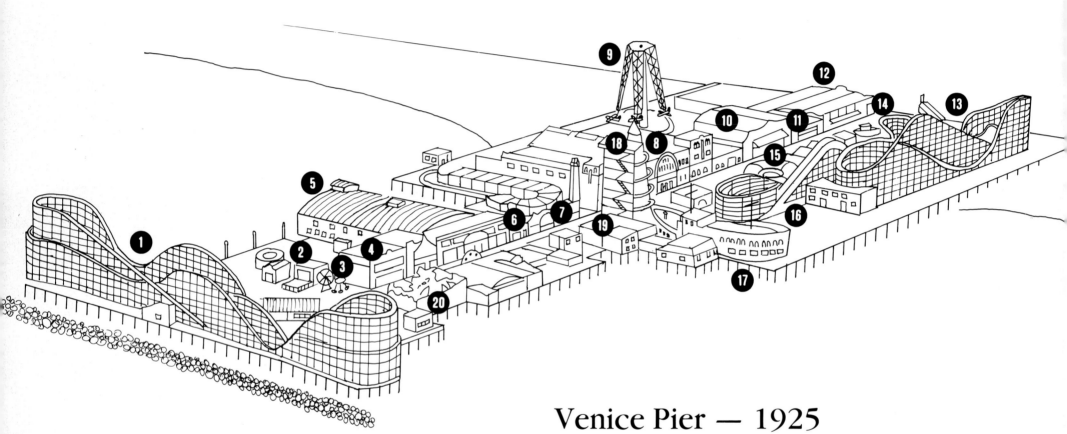

Venice Pier — 1925

1. Some Kick Roller Coaster
2. Automatic Baseball Game
3. Kiddie Rides
4. Glass House
5. Fun House
6. Shooting Gallery
7. Flying Circus Entrance
8. Dance Hall
9. Flying Circus
10. Mery-go-round (Dentzel)
11. Skee Ball
12. Billiards & Bowling
13. Giant Dipper Roller Coaster
14. Noah's Ark
15. Great American Racing Derby
16. Bob's Roller Coaster
17. Ship's Cafe
18. Dragon Bamboo Slide
19. Over the Falls
20. Coal Mine

Aerial looking south shows Center Street Pier and much larger Venice Pier; 1925.

The Venice Pier midway looking west shows the newly constructed Dragon Bamboo Slide. The Bobs entrance is on the left and the Dance Hall is on the right; 1926.

The midway on the Venice Pier featured rides and concessions. The Giant Dipper and Bob roller coasters are on the left, Some Kick coaster is at the end of the pier; 1924. (left)

The Venice Pier midway looking east shows the Fun House and the back of the Dragon Bamboo Slide; 1928.

A view, looking east, of the Venice Pier midway. The Coal Mine ride is on the far right, and behind it is the Ship Cafe; 1925. (right)

the dance floor and keep them separate from the new group coming onto the floor. Single girls would watch from the side until an eligible male would ask them to dance, while couples who came together usually occupied the loges.

Venice' first spring as part of Los Angeles was a quiet one, until the disappearance of evangelist Aimee Sempre McPherson thrust it into the national limelight. She checked into her suite at the Ocean View Hotel on May 18, 1926. Then she and her secretary walked to the beach. Aimee waded into the surf while her secretary read a bible. When she failed to return an intensive search making national headlines was launched.

Airplanes and deepsea divers were called into the search. Thousands of "Sister Aimee's" followers came to the beach to help and to pray. One mourner committed suicide and a lifeguard drowned during the search for her body.

Of course it was rumored that local amusement interests were involved in foul play. The evangelist had advocated a referendum to ban Sunday dancing in Venice.

A month later they held a memorial service at Venice beach. Then two days later Aimee reappeared outside Douglas, Arizona, and told a tale of kidnapping, torture, and escape across the Mexican desert. When contradictions in her story surfaced, charges were filed against her for obstructing justice. However, prosecution was suddenly halted, and all charges against the evangelist were dropped in 1927.

Ocean Park amusement interests enjoyed the unexpected publicity and as usual prepared for the busy summer season by adding new attractions to their Ocean Park Pier. The Whip and Scooter rides were placed between the Merry-go-round building and the Dome Theater. Other new attractions in 1926 included the Pig Slide, Freak Slide Show, Captive Aeroplanes, Tango and Rabit Racer.

One of the most unusual attractions added that year was the 'Chinatown and the Underworld' waxworks. Each of the 29 separate exhibits, designed by F.R. Glass of New York City, featured realistic scenes such as McGurk's suicide hall in the Bowery, a Chinese opium den and a wedding showing slave girls and tong hatchet men. Underworld scenes included gambling dens with the capture of drug smugglers, an electrocution at Sing Sing, crimes in the Parisian sewers, Brooklyn's black hand kidnapper's in action, the Furnail murder and several dramatically portrayed beheading and torture scenes. They was a complete replica of the noted New

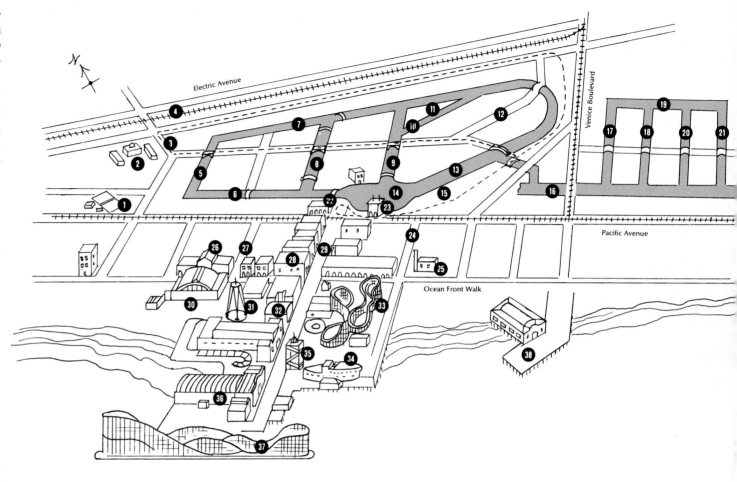

1. Club House Country Club
2. Central School now Westminster School
3. Miniature Railroad route
4. Electric Trolley "Red Car" route
5. Venus Canal, now San Juan Avenue
6. Coral Canal, now Main Street
7. Cabrillo Canal
8. Aldebaran Canal, now Market Street
9. Lion Canal, now Windward Avenue
10. Altair Canal
11. U.S. Island
12. Rialto Street
13. Grand Canal, now Grand Boulevard
14. Venice Lagoon, now traffic circle
15. Site of "Race Thru the Clouds"
16. Grand Canal extension
17. Carroll Canal
18. Linnie Canal
19. Eastern Canal
20. Howland Canal
21. Sherman Canal
22. Site of Bathhouse on Venice Lagoon
23. Site of Amphitheater, now Post Office
24. Loreli Street

Aerial view of the rebuilt Venice Pier and the Venice of America canals; 1925. (opposite page)

Giant Dipper

OCEAN SIDE

ICE CREAM SODAS

THIS IS SURE SOME FICKLE RIDE

The Giant Dipper roller coaster replaced the Big Dipper coaster on the Venice Pier in 1924.

The Flying Circus was a spectacular aerial ride. Its six, eight passenger cars circled the main tower 65 feet above the pier, and performed aerial stunts that convinced passengers that they were actually airborne, 1925.

VENICE BATHING BEAUTY PARA
SUNDAY-MAY. 17 · 1925.

York City Mott and Tyler streets inside. The entire wax exhibit was a work of art.

Ocean Park held their Mardi Gras festival and water carnival over the Fourth of July weekend. The three day festival climaxed with a presentation of 'Ocean Park on Fire', a grand fireworks display that held spectators spellbound. Apparently tourists who missed last year's fire could watch a reenactment of the disaster in miniature.

Ocean Park's parades and celebrations during the twenties were an alternative to those of rival Venice, somewhat offbeat and different. While the Children's Floral Parade had been an annual event since 1920, the Male Beauty Parade was first staged in the late twenties. Males of every type from Hollywood Shieks with oily pomaded hair to big he-men competed for the $300 in prize money. There were burly men and puny men, ones that were fat and short, others that were tall and lean. There were prizes for the most perfect figure, most handsome male, most athletic male, homeliest male, and even a comic division.

In September the Los Angeles Surf Club subleased the recently closed Sunset Pier from the Electric Pier Company. They presented plans to the city for a first class club house that would encompass five city blocks of ocean front property adjacent to the pier. A new ballroom with a capacity of 4000 dancers would be built on the pier. This as usual became just another pier project that became financially insolvent.

The Los Angeles Parks Department acquired $4500 worth of boats and canoes from private interests in November. They decided, especially if they could make a profit, to promote boating on the canals while the canal court case dragged on. They also built a lifeguard station on the beach at Brooks Avenue. A $500,000 bond issue for beach improvements was placed on the spring 1927 ballot, but it was to be subsequently defeated.

Venice's various civic organizations, especially the local branch of the Chamber of Commerce, supported the Kinney Company's plans to build a new business district on the old Villa City site near the Grand Canal. That fall All 246 vacation villas were vacated and razed. It was an era when openings of newly paved roads and monthly records for building permits made front page news. The Venice Vanguard newspaper editorials constantly advocated progress.

When Judge Henry Hollzer of the California Supreme Court confirmed in December that the municipality had the power to fill in the canals, Thornton Kinney issued a statement. "Venice was a dream city and without

Pacific Electric trolley cars on Trolley Way at Windward; 1929. (above)

The miniature railroad served as a local transportation system around the Venice canals. The turnaround point was at Windward and Pacific; 1924.

New Years Day celebration on the Venice Pier; 1928. (left)

Windward Avenue at night; 1925.

sentiment it could not be built. But financial calculations suffocate sentiment and the march of time and progress of the community demanded sentiment be stifled."

By March the new lagoon business district was nearly ready. Workers were pouring concrete for the streets, and the Kinney Company announced that a $300,000 hotel would be built there. With the canals scheduled to be filled and paved by the end of the year, it appeared to some people that Venice was finally modernizing.

The Kinney Company, as they usually did each spring, improved their pier. Five new attractions were added. Former deep sea diver Harry Behrens opened an aquarium on the seaward side of the Dragon Slide. Others added the Submarine Divers, Temptation, and a wax exhibit called 20 Years in Sing Sing. And now that the Flying Circus was loading passengers directly below the tall turret, the old entrance station and track became part of a dark ride called the Flying Trains.

Some of the craziness of the roaring twenties hit Venice that spring. Dance marathons became the fad and dance halls everywhere were offering big cash prizes for the couple that could dance the longest. There were five minute breaks every hour for participants to go to the bathroom or grab something to eat, but in general they danced till they dropped of exhaustion. Officials stopped one dance marathon at the Venice Dance Hall after 21 hours - the ten remaining couples divided the $1000 prize equally.

Sometimes the dance marathons run by big promoters took to the streets. In one such event couples danced their way from the Venice Dance Hall to the El Patio Ballroom in downtown Los Angeles. City officials soon confined the contests to single sites.

During the summer the city council intended to proceed with filling in the canals. They legally changed the canal names to streets, then passed a canal fill order that was to be paid for by an assessment to the area. They claimed that only 62 people out of 7500 property owners in the assessment district protested. On Dec 12, 1927 they awarded the canal fill contract to the R. A. Wattson Company.

Although the contract had been signed, the Board of Public Works refused to execute it in January 1928. Since the canals had been dedicated to the old city by Abbot Kinney, with the condition that they be used "solely and only for permanent waterways and canals, free to the public forever", the board feared that if the canals were filled in they would revert to the Kinney heirs.

Entrance to Some Kick roller coaster on the Venice Pier; 1928.

Wattson took his case to court because he wanted to proceed with the work without legal hindrance. A petition for a writ of mandate was filed, but the District Court of Appeals refused it on Dec 18, 1928 on the grounds that the canals were dedicated to the city as waterways and they could not be legally used for any other purpose. With no recourse, the contractor took his case to the the California Supreme Court, which ruled in the contractor's favor. The court stated that the waterways were transportation corridors and although Kinney did not anticipate newer modes of transportation, it was no reason to deny their use to such vehicles. It also ruled that the property owners had no vested interests because the canals were artificial.

Despite a gala three day canal filling celebration attended by Governor C.C. Young and five thousand residents, it was a dark day in Venice's history that summer of '29 when the first trucks pulled up beside Coral Canal, now Main Street, to dump the first loads of dirt. It was almost directly in front of the postmaster's house that an angry crowd of over a hundred jumped into the drained canal and started shoveling the dirt out almost as fast as the contractor's crew could fill it in.

Nonetheless work was completed before the end of the year at a cost of $636,205.85. Nearly 90,000 cubic yards of dirt were trucked in, rolled flat and covered by a seven inch layer of asphaltic concrete. The contractor installed a central drain basin and pumping plant beneath Kinney Plaza sufficient to handle 9,160 feet of storm drains. Its five huge pumps were more than capable of handling the area's water runoff.

The other canals south of Venice Boulevard remained. It is said that they were saved by the depression and the contractor's bankruptcy. But in truth, the area, which was only half developed, wouldn't have supported an assessment. That and the lack of need for more roads saved the remaining canals.

The roaring twenties ended with one last pier expansion in Ocean Park. In April 1929 E.P. King, general manager of Ocean Park Realty Corporation, announced $3,000,000 worth of improvements to the Ocean Park Pier. They lengthened the pier 500 feet and built five new buildings and attractions.

Foremost was C.L. Langley's $150,000 Shoot the Shoots ride at the very end of the pier. It was the highest amusement chute ever built, and the only one on a pier. The 56 foot wide pool at the bottom contained 150,000 tons of water. Although the ride first appeared back in 1895 at Sea Lion Park in Coney Island and was a standard feature at most amusement parks, it wasn't built in the

Ship Cafe on the rebuilt Venice Pier faced the ocean parallel to the beach; 1929.

United States Island; 1926. In this view looking north, Altair Canal is on the left, Cabrillo Canal on the right. (above)

Venice / Ocean Park area until concrete piers were built strong enough to support its huge weight.

Flat bottom boats would make a thrilling descent down a 120 foot high 30 degree sloped water runway into a three feet deep pool. In charge of every boatload of passengers was a competent oarsman whose duty was to bring the boat to the landing stage after the boat ran out of momentum. They stood erect in the rear of the boat and maintained their balance with one heavy single oar in hand as the craft struck water at the bottom and bounded in the air. When the boat stopped the oarsman sculled it to one side of the pond where passengers landed.

Filling in the canals along Grand Canal and the lagoon area.

Other rides installed nearby were a Ferris Wheel with seats in pairs facing each other, some kiddie rides and an Aero Glider. Jone's Fun Palace on Ocean Front Walk was converted into a roller skating rink.

Numerous new changes were made to the Venice Pier amusement zone. They removed the Bobs roller coaster when Fred Church moved to New York City and put in a flat circular Hey Dey ride where the coaster's old entrance stood. The old merry-go-round building next to the Dance Hall was razed for space for a new midway. The Parker carousel from Jones' Fun Palace was moved to the new area and installed under a tent behind Harry Hargrave's Niagara Barrel, then under construction.

The $50,000 ride consisted of a 25 foot diameter glass barrel suspended between two steel structural towers resting in a fountain base 45 feet in diameter. An escalator conveyed passengers to the top of the plat-form where they entered the barrel. Inside was a slightly smaller barrel set at a 25 degree angle which rocked back and forth and rotated counter-clockwise. The outer barrel rotated in the opposite direction while water cascaded over it in a fountain effect. Passengers, losing all sense of direction, imagined that they were being turned over or somersaulted in mid-air as if they were going over Niagara Falls in a barrel.

A Lindy Loop ride was placed out near the end of the pier. The ride, built in Chicago, had two counter balanced tubular shaped cars that were suspended from a 65 foot high horizontal supported shaft. The operator, controlling a pair of rheostats, caused powerful oppos-ing motors attached to the shaft to rock the cars back and forth until they gradually climbed and looped overhead like airplanes. One car would loop clockwise while the other looped counter-clockwise. If the operator was clever he could get the cars stuck overhead and shake it until the passengers lost the money in their pockets.

The city took possession of the Sunset Pier in the spring after the lease was cancelled with the Electric Pier Company for nonpayment of rent. By that time the superstructure was gone and they only needed to remove the pilings to finish demolition. However, in June the Parks and Recreation Commission decided to build a 64 x 160 foot municipal bathing pavilion on the pier. The pool, costing $20,000, could accomodate 3000 people and would have large sun rooms. Con-struction would begin by the end of the year despite the beginning of the economic downturn initiated by the stock market crash in late October.

Loreli Street, now 17th Street, one block south of Windward, housed the police and fire stations.

CHAPTER 6

Oil, Depression & War Years (1930-1945)

Venice entered the Depression in the midst of hope and despair. On the one hand the economic downturn caused by the stock market crash and the subsequent failure of the banking industry meant little disposable income for the amusement industry. On the other hand the discovery of oil held the possibilities of untold wealth for the community.

The Ohio Oil Company brought in a wildcat well on December 18, 1929 in Del Rey on county property just east of the Grand Canal at Avenue 35. The well initially produced 3000 barrels per day of deep sand oil from a depth of 6199 feet. The triumphant company then asked for a zoning variance that would permit them to drill for oil within the city limits on the Venice Peninsula.

The town's excitement soon turned to oil fever. Parcels of land and mineral rights rapidly traded hands. Residents talked of nothing but oil and the money that could be made by having an oil well in one's backyard. On January 9, 1930 a crowd of 2000 met with officials at the old City Hall and demanded re-zoning to allow oil drilling. Nearly 95% of the residents were in favor of the change. Ocean Park residents, however, weren't so lucky. Santa Monica was strictly against drilling.

Los Angeles city planners lifted the oil drilling ban on January 28th but were cautious and only allowed drilling south of Lenona (Washington Street). They set up rules allowing a maximum of two wells per city block, then issued 15 permits. Two weeks later the City Council rubber stamped the permits.

The Ohio Oil Company began drilling their second well in March and struck oil on May 3rd. It was a small well that produced only 1500 barrels per day. Owners of Star #1 were luckier a month later when their well at Avenue 35 and the Grand Canal came in at 5000 barrels per day. By June the payroll in the oil field was $75,000 per week.

By late September, when nearly 50 wells were in operation, the oil field was ranked sixth in the state. The fashionable and promising residential district had turned into a noisy, smelly, ugly and dangerous area. Oil waste was constantly being dumped into the canal and lagoon, and an explosion only a month before destroyed

The Venice Traffic Circle replaced the lagoon area after the canals were filled. The pumping plant for the storm drains is under the center of the traffic circle. (above)

Oil was discovered on the Venice Peninsula in 1929. By August 1930 when this aerial was taken, there were over one hundred oil derricks pumping or exploring for oil. This area is the strand in front of the Marina del Rey harbor. (opposite page)

One of the most popular attractions on the Venice Pier was the Fun House. Inside were slides, a miniature roller coaster, rotating barrels, two spinning Society Wheels, a Mystery Room, curved mirrors and the Fun House Bus.

Spinning Society Wheel hurls people off inside Fun House.

one oil drilling rig. The city closed the Florence Nightingale School on the peninsula for safety and transferred the children to other schools. Though they sought restrictions to protect the beach and tidelands from drilling, it was too late. The beach was already polluted.

The oil field was so successful that by the end of the year oil company owners planned to curtail production to stabilize prices. A local gas price war had lowered prices to eight cents per gallon and profits were down. The 148 operating oil wells were producing at a rate of 46,932 barrels and 2,000,000 cu ft of gas daily. The Venice oil field had become the 4th largest oil field in the state. Unfortunately the field was soon depleted and by early 1932 oil production dropped way down.

Despite the economic cushion provided by the oil business, the amusement business began to suffer that first summer of the Depression. There were only a few improvements made to Venice's amusement zone - a Monkey Zoo featuring several hundred monkeys opened just beyond the Fun House and the Motordrome located near the pier entrance was moved to the ocean end. And in the following year, only two new kiddie rides were opened, the Juvenile Circus and the Toyland Riding Academy.

Women try to prevent their dresses from being blown upward by hidden air jets inside the Fun House.

129

With spending money becoming scarce and money for new attractions non-existent, amusement men resorted to promotions and celebrations to lure paying customers to Venice and Ocean Park. The schedule for 1931 included the St. Patrick's Day parade, Easter Fashion Pageant, Pacific Memorial Day services, Fiesta Week in June, Independence Day with fireworks, Annual Bathing Revue, Mermaid Mardi Gras in August, Labor Day celebration, Halloween Carnival, Armistice Day celebration, 1st Annual Turkey Trot, two week long Christmas Fiesta and the 24th annual New Year's Eve Frolic.

Amusement interests were fortunate that summer as the crowds at the beach were larger than in the previous two years and water temperatures hovered between a record 76 and 78 degrees Fahrenheit, only a degree or two colder than the waters off Hawaii. Hammerhead sharks were sighted in the bay for the first time. World wide weather was bizarre that summer; extreme heat and drought in North America with record rain through-out Europe. Inland Los Angeles temperatures hovered around the 100 degree mark throughout the summer and residents headed for the beach to escape the heat. Sunday's July 26th crowd that packed the narrow beach solid from Del Rey to the Ocean Park Pier was estimated at 350,000 people. Five hundred people took a late evening swim by moonlight near the pier. The only discomfort was the swarms of mosquitoes that plagued Venice throughout the summer.

The Venice Ballroom celebrated its 25th anniversary. Although it had enough business on weekends, it offered free dancing on weekdays. The place was packed nearly every night with couples doing the jitterbug, lindy hop, rumba and slow fox trot.

The pier's amusement rides were considered safe, but on August 13th there was bizarre accident on the Ocean Park Pier's Hi-Boy roller coaster. The front car became uncoupled from the rest of the train and didn't make it to the top of the next hill. The empty rear cars, with much less momentum, stopped near the bottom. When the front car, rolling backwards, struck the rest of the train at the bottom, its four passengers were hurled backwards out of their seats to land in the empty car behind. It was a lucky accident or they might have fallen between the rails to their deaths.

Others weren't always so lucky. There were always signs posted warning passengers "Do not stand up!" One teenager, no doubt showing off to his friends, disobeyed the warning sign when Some Kick coaster first opened in 1923 and had his head smashed in by a protruding post. Over the years some stood up and were hurled out of the cars on sharp turns, only to land on the pier far below or sometimes in the ocean. Most were drunk, but a few did it on a dare. One kid tried to ride a coaster unseated, hanging on to the restraining bar by his hands alone. He lost his grip on a fast turn and died when he struck the pier pilings below.

Many consider 1932 the worst year of the depression. Banks like the First National Bank of Venice and Ocean Park's Marine Bank were failing in record numbers, and jobs were scarce everywhere. But Los Angeles was preparing for the 10th Olympiad and the Venice / Ocean Park amusement interests intended to take advantage of it. They planned to lure the Olympic crowd with 25 cent Pacific Electric roundtrip excursion fares on Wednesdays and Sundays.

In May the Southern California water polo team, composed mostly of Venice swimmers, won the west coast championship. Five Venice men including Wally O'Conner (captain), Phil Daubenspeck, Charles Finn, Herb Wildman and Bill O'Conner won positions on the United States water polo team. The team upset Brazil and Japan in the playoffs and tied Germany 4-4 in the semi-finals. But in the August 11th final match, they lost to Hungary 7-0.

Venice held some interesting events that summer. July 4th festivities included a daredevil's descent by parachute while operating a fireworks show. Louis 'Speedy' Babbs leaped from a plane at 8000 feet with bombs strapped to his body and a brand in his teeth. Unfortunately, one of the bombs prematurely exploded and his clothes caught fire at 5000 feet. Spectators didn't realize what had happened until his writhing body, enveloped in flames, dropped out of the fog into the clear a few hundred feet above the ocean where speed boats quickly rescued him. He was hospitalized with first and second degree burns.

Beauty contests evolved from local contests to state-wide pageants. Venice held a contest on July 25, 1932 to select Miss California at the Venice Ballroom. The media covered it live by radio.

A strong indication that pier business dropped off sharply occurred that fall. In October the Abbot Kinney Company shocked the confidence of concessionaires and others when they defaulted on bond interest payments. It was only a year earlier that the company had sold $350,000 in new bonds to raise capital to retire maturing bonds. The company was then operated by an appointed receiver, Edward Gerety Jr., son of a former mayor of Venice.

While few people were spending money on amusement rides, they were spending it on bingo or at least a variation of the popular game. Bingo was considered a gambling game and therefore was illegal in Los Angeles. However, the clever game operators invented variations that allowed the customer to use their "skill" to select the numbers called. This might involve tossing marbles in a grid, or rolling balls down an incline. Game cards costing a nickle to a quarter, depending on the number of players, offered prizes of $1.50 to $50.00.

One of the most successful operators was John Harrah and his son Bill. The former Venice mayor was badly in debt after the stock market crash, yet owned mortgages on a number of beach properties far above their deflated value. One such property was the Plaza Building at the entrance to the Venice Pier. At the time it housed mostly bowling alleys and a pool hall. They decided to use the part of the empty space to open up a variation of bingo which they called the 'Circle Game'. Players sat at a large circular style bar during the game and marked their bingo cards. A revolving game board with its connecting runway was placed in the center. Each player in turn determined the next number by rolling a ball down the runway so that it landed into one of the numbered slots. The 32 seat parlor grossed $100 the first night it opened on July 4, 1932. The Harrahs were so successful that they soon opened a second game called Tango, then a third.

By 1934 the state passed a law outlawing bingo as a game of chance at his parlors and others that lined the coast. The police and county sheriffs raided the games to shut them down. The arresting officer became confused when Harrah's game didn't even look like bingo. They managed to stay open nearly six months after everyone else was closed by constantly changing the games and keeping one step ahead of the law.

The legality of the games were constantly challenged in court, but there were still periodic raids and closures in 1935 and 1936. While Harrah became fed up with the constant legal trials and uncertainties and moved to Reno in 1937, others evolved the game into a variation called Bridgo. It lasted until after World War II when a final courtroom test closed the "games of skill" for good.

Natural disasters in 1933 and 1934 did almost as much to damage Venice as the Depression did. The Long Beach earthquake on March 10, 1933 wrecked the high school auditorium and damaged a number of build-ings. The second story of the Security Pacific Bank build-ing at Trolley Way and Windward had to be removed to

Venice Pier midway at night; 1938.

make the structure safe.

Then in January 1934 heavy rains caused Ballona Creek and the Grand Canal to overflow and flood Venice. The Sunset Pier was used as a relief center for the 1400 families that had to evacuate their homes. Afterwards the community wanted to fill in the remaining canals, but the estimated cost of $185,000 was a frivolous expense during the Depression. The Works Progress Administration did, however, begin work on building a flood control levee on Ballona Creek the following year. It helped but failed to curtain the brunt of the 1938 flood.

Congress passed the Little Volsted Act on April 7, 1933 as a prelude to ending Prohibition. It authorized the consumption of 3.2% beer in any municipality that would allow it. Los Angeles put the issue on the May ballot and it passed. Shortly afterwards a beer garden opened on the end of the Venice Pier. The Ship Cafe, now able to sell beer, remodeled and reopened under the ownership of Tommy Jacob. By the end of the year the states ratified the repeal of the 21st Amendment, and it became legal once again to drink liquor on December 5, 1933.

Dance marathons were popular on the Venice Pier from the late 20's through the 30's. Contestants competing for prize money, danced till they dropped.

In August the Halper-Robbins Corporation proposed to build a $3.5 million amusement project between Avenue 17 and Avenue 34. It would have a huge yacht harbor protected by a 1400 foot sea wall, a 1500 foot long concrete amusement pier, a ballroom and a 150 foot tall observation tower. The owners were seeking financing from an Eastern backer.

But L.A. Councilman Charles W. Breedlove was seeking political support for his own improvement plans for the beach area. He sought federal money to build a series of jetties, a seawall, breakwater, yacht club, aquarium and other facilities. He was dead set against a private corporation building what he thought the government could do better.

Venetians were becoming more frequently dissatisfied with Los Angeles city government. They were forced to grapple with a government bureaucracy physically remote and preoccupied with ameliorating the economic effects of the Depression. While they expected a fair shake after annexation, it seemed all they got were increased property taxes and little service in return. Property taxes increased by 116% from 1923 to 1929, yet not one bond issue for local improvements was approved by the electorate during the first few years after annexation. Bond issues for a community clubhouse and auditorium were regularly defeated. Venice did obtain a new police headquarters, library and municipal swimming pool, but not until 1930.

Some suggested secession from Los Angeles. Secessionists managed to get 12,000 signatures on petitions asking for a state constitutional amendment to hold a special election within the old incorporated city. Assemblyman Ernest O. Voight authored the amendment and it passed the Assembly, 54 to 13, on June 14, 1935. The bill then went to the Senate where powerful lobbyists from the Los Angeles Department of Water & Power attempted to defeat it. Unfortunately for Venice, they were able to delay it just long enough for the Senate to adjourn before action could be taken on the bill.

Business conditions on the Venice Pier during the summer were the best they had been in the previous four or five years. The biggest reason was the reduction of Pacific Electric's roundtrip fare from fifty five cents to thirty-five cents. This enabled more large families to afford to come to the beach. Pier concessionaires also sponsored 'Five Cent Days' for children on Wednesday afternoons. Kids could ride any one of eight of their favorite rides for half price. Rooms were starting to get scarce.

Aerial view looking north shows the Sunset Municipal Pier, Venice Pier, and Ocean Park Pier; 1941.

Venice held its first annual Mardi Gras Festival August 16-18, 1935. The three day event, featuring parades, costumes, contests and entertainment, was modeled after the New Orleans event. It was conceived by the local businessmen as a commercial enterprise that would publicize the community, attract large crowds and require the cooperation of people from many segments of the populace.

It began with the arrival of King Neptune, Queen Venetia's coronation and a royal procession along Ocean Front Walk. The queen read a proclamation commanding her subjects to engage in three days of fun and frivolity. The afternoon parade featured floats, bands and costumed merrymakers wearing enormous plaster of paris heads. Windward Avenue was roped off for a street carnival where wandering gondoliers entertained.

There was an afternoon treasure hunt for children and an evening program of aquatic events on Saturday. Sunday's Miss California beauty pageant drew huge crowds, and a Mardi Gras Ball in the evening capped the celebration.

The Mardi Gras Festival became an annual event of considerable importance prior to World War II. It became bigger and better each succeeding year and civic pride improved. By 1941 five hundred thousand people attended the expanded four day event in its final year.

The Venice Surfing Club gained prominence during the time of the Mardi Gras festivals. Its thirty to forty members, mostly teens and young adults, met at a small clubhouse on the end of the Sunset Pier. It was first formed as a paddleboard club in the early 30's, but when members like Louigi Varlucchi, Tom Wilde, Ed Adams, Tom Blake and Tully Clark began shaping the big wooden boards and experimenting with unmovable rudders placed on the tail, most members began to surf. Lifeguards reserved half of the the beach area between Sunset Pier and the Venice Pier exclusively for surfboards and paddleboards.

Venice began to recover from the Depression after 1935. Business conditions improved, primarily because of the success of the Douglas Aircraft Company in Santa Monica, which was busy making DC-3's. Workers seeking housing and families who were staying in Venice through the winter because of higher rents inland caused a housing shortage. Garages were converted into living quarters and single family residences were converted to multi-family.

In 1937 Joe Semper, a store owner on Windward, spearheaded a drive to remodel the street in order to

Mardi Gras Parade along Windward Avenue; 1938.

Mardi Gras Parade. King Neptune and Queen Veneita lead the parade along Ocean Front Walk. (opposite page)

Surfing was popular during the late 1930's between the Sunset Municipal Pier and the Venice Pier.

attract more business. The exteriors of the buildings were restuccoed and colorful neon lighting was installed along the colonnade's arches and rooflines of the buildings.

While the Kinney Company had little money to refurbish their pier, some concessionaires risked scarce capital for new rides. In 1935 an Octopus ride was installed on the vacated open area where the old Hey Dey stood. It in turn was replaced by a Strataship in 1938, an aerial ride that lasted only a year. Rudy Illions, who was busy building Scooter rides after his family's carousel company in Coney Island closed in 1929 due to financial difficulties, installed one across from Leninger's Salt Water Taffy in the building east of the Niagara Barrel. It was a bumper car ride with the steering adjusted so the cars couldn't travel backwards. The tented Parker carousel behind the Niagara Barrel was moved into a vacant building across the midway in 1931 and remained there until it was sold in 1939. Some Kick rollercoaster was removed after the 1934 season but nothing replaced it.

Likewise, the Ocean Park Pier offered the public minimal improvements until the last half of the Depression. Mike Allmah's Reptile Garden opened in 1936 at the end of the Ocean Park Pier and a Waltzer ride was installed the following year. It resembled the Whip, but the ride was more circular and the cars looked like Model T's. In 1938 Ed Martine's Diving Bell began operation just inland of the Chutes, and Rudy Illions built another Skooter ride next door to his Looff carousel.

The old Egyptian Dance Hall, which had been vacant for some time, became the Sportland Arcade in 1939. The same season Venice Pier's Lindy Loop was moved adjacent to the Hi-Boy coaster and the Fun in the Dark ride next to the Whip began a run that lasted two years. Its cars, travelling on rails through narrow passageways, transported people past things that would jump out at them. It was meant to be a scary ride. The Bug House, a mirror maze style fun house, replaced it just prior to the war.

Two aerial-type rides were placed in the large open area seaward of the Toonerville Fun House. The Spitfire, built by the Everly Aircraft Company in Salem Oregon, placed both opposing counterweighted planes at ends of a rotating rigid beam that was canted on a 45 degree axis. The pilot of each plane used a control stick to operate the plane's ailerons. Once the plane reached air speed, he could perform 360 degree barrel rolls or fly straight and level in a circle along the beam's tilted axis. On the other hand, the Roll-O-Plane's two opposing

Aerial view of the Venice Pier in 1941 shows some of the changes that occurred during the late 20's and the Depression. Both the Bobs and Some Kick roller coasters are gone, the Palace Building is where Noah's Ark stood, and the Niagara Barrel occupies the site where the carousel building stood.

cars rotated directly overhead. This would have turned the passengers completely upside down at the top, except that the two back-to-back passenger compartments rolled as the ride rotated. Passengers would become dizzy and disoriented but they never were completely upside down.

The late 30's brought back the popularity of the offshore gambling boats. A fleet of these boats began in 1929 with the operation of the Tango anchored five miles directly west of the Venice Pier. Water taxis would deposit gamblers at these floating casinos that sometimes offered entertainment and dancing in addition to crap tables and roulette.

In 1938 Tony Cornero converted a 41 year old brigantine into a gambling ship. It had a superstructure especially designed as a luxury gambling casino. His investment, rumored to be $600,000, was financed by Bugsy Siegal and George Raft. He towed his boat exactly 3.1 miles offshore, and announced with radio and newspaper advertisements that he was open for business. He offered a challenge, a $100,000 reward to anyone who could show that any game on the Rex was rigged.

It was a first class operation with good food, top name dance bands, unwatered booze and honest games. Gamblers had a choice of playing craps, roulette, blackjack, chuck-a-luck, high spade, wheel of fortune, chinese lottery, stud poker and faro. There were Tango layouts between decks and 150 'one-armed bandits' lined the casino walls. Nick the Greek Dandolos, Carl Leemmle, and Fanny Brice were noted celebrity gamblers that added atmosphere to the floating casino. The operation was a success and netted Tony $300,000 per month.

The Rex and other gambling ships were a thorn in the side of anti-gambling forces. The local authorities could do nothing because they operated just beyond their jurisdiction. Police often harrassed the water taxi service, but their efforts were struck down in court. Finally California Attorney General Earl Warren decided to take action. He armed himself with nuisance abatement warrants and went after the gambling fleet.

He had no difficulty in shutting down two boats in Long Beach and the Texas off Venice, but the Rex didn't give in easily. Cornero got wind of the operation when seventeen unarmed plainclothes officers tried to sneak aboard the ship with the other customers. Bouncers spotted them easily and escorted them off the ship.

Warren rounded up a flotilla of State and Game boats, manned them with deputies and ordered them out to the Rex. Cornero was ready and repelled the invasion with high-pressure fire hoses. The authorities laid siege for nine tense days while Cornero's men stood guard with sub-machine guns. His attorneys filed suit after suit charging Warren with everything from harrassment to piracy.

Then Tony Conero unexpectedly surrendered on August 9, 1938. The war moved to the courts. The high court finally ruled a year later that the three mile limit in the Santa Monica Bay extended from an imaginary line connecting Point Dume to Point Vicente. Tony had to pay fines and court costs.

America prepared for war in 1941. The draft was enacted and nearly 200 local youth were serving in the armed forces when hostilities broke out on December 7, 1941. Venice residents suddenly found themselves in the first line of defense.

A blackout was immediately instituted, and National Guardsmen patrolled the beach. Helmeted air raid wardens took their duties seriously as they inspected their blocks nightly for any stray shaft of light that might become a beacon for enemy warships and subs. The Douglas Aircraft factory was completely camouflaged so that it looked like a harmless housing tract from the air.

Venetians who remained on the home front worked in war factories or tended their 'victory gardens'. Others did volunteer work with the USO and Red Cross or helped civic organizations with their war bond drives. Everyone felt the effects of rationing.

The amusement piers were open throughout the war except at night. Soldiers and sailors came to the piers and boardwalk on weekend leaves. Some tried their luck at a game on the end of the Venice Pier called Dump Mable Out of Bed. It was one of those games where a baseball was thrown at a target, and if hit would drop someone in a tub of water. However, this was a sexier version. Girls wearing nighties would lie in bed while sailors threw the ball in an attempt to roll them out of bed into the water below. Another attraction that seemed to fascinate them was the Wall of Death. George True rode a motorcycle around the inside of a huge metal cage.

Dancing was a favorite way to meet local girls. Harry James and Benny Goodman played swing music at the Casino Gardens on the Ocean Park Pier. The Venice Dance Hall offered country western music by the best bands in the west.

By 1943, threats of invasion had diminished sufficiently to permit near normal operation of the amusement zone during the evening hours. The piers were also a

haven for young Mexican-Americans who adopted a style of dress distinctly their own. The boys wore duck-tail haircuts, flat pancake hats, peg-top trousers, reet pleets, long glittering watch chains and long drape coats. The girls, dubbed "cholitas" wore tight fitting sweaters and black hobble skirts that stopped above the kneeline. Going out in your best attire was called "zooting".

It was inevitable that tension would develop between the 'zoot suiters' and the servicemen that congregated at the piers on weekend nights. On the night of May 8, 1943 rumors circulated along the beach that one of the 'zoot-suiters' had knifed a sailor and a clash began. Several hundred soldiers, sailors and local teenagers ran the Mexican-Americans out of the Aragon Ballroom on the Lick Pier. They clashed again after midnight along Ocean Front Walk at Navy Street in front of a crowd of 2500 spectators. Thirteen 'zoot-suiters' were arrested and 28 more were taken into custody following the battle.

A short while later the Merchants Building on the Ocean Front Walk and Windward mysteriously caught fire. The Kinney Company's offices along with nine other businesses and 18 automobiles in the garage were destroyed. Police suspected arson since witnesses reported two male "zoot-suiters" were seen hanging around the building before the fire. Their motive was revenge for the arrests of their friends.

The stage was set for another round of fighting the following weekend. Police roadblocks intercepted over a hundred "zoot-suiters" bound for Venice, and arrested eight local youths who were discovered carrying concealed weapons. It ended the Venice wars but the clashes soon moved to downtown Los Angeles where worse racial violence took place.

The war years weren't very good for Venice. In 1943 the California State Board of Health quarantined the beach as far north as Brooks Avenue because Los Angeles was dumping raw sewage into Santa Monica Bay. Then Los Angeles officials closed the Plunge because dry rot in the structure over the pool made it unsafe. Wartime restrictions on building material had prevented repair.

The war ended on August 14, 1945. The residents were ecstatic and celebrated throughout the amusement districts. Everyone was looking forward to reuniting their families and building a new life. The amusement people were hoping to attract new business by remodeling their piers, a job that would take money and time.

CHAPTER 7

Dismantling of Venice (1946-1972)

The Kinney Company's 25 year lease on the Venice Pier expired on January 13, 1946. Leo H. Strickland, manager of the company, was dumbfounded when his landlord, the City of Los Angeles Parks and Recreation Department, declined to renew the lease. The company had put in a new pier entrance only the previous fall at a cost of $60,000 and reinforced and resurfaced the pier near the Ship Cafe. It was a profitable business with revenues of $100,000 annually and there was no question that they expected to renew the pier's lease after the war. The amusement business was Venice's bread and butter industry, and now that the war was over it was the key to the community's return to prosperity.

But the officials of the Parks and Recreation department were firm about not renewing the lease because the pier conflicted with their master plan. They expected to widen the beach soon and wanted all structures jutting out into the ocean removed. Long range plans also included construction of an inland yacht harbor at Del Rey, and possibly a relocated amusement zone.

The Kinney Company tried to negotiate an extension of their $1000 a month lease, at least through the busy summer season. But the Parks Department, claiming that they were flooded with Venice residents asking that the Kinney lease not be renewed, gave them one month to remove their pier concessions effective March 16, 1946. Many Venice property owners were certain that property values would rise once the pier was razed.

City councilman Edward Davenport made a recommendation at the March 24th meeting to postpone the dismantlement of the pier until March 1, 1947, a time when the pier would then interfere with the beach widening project. He felt that "Premature destruction of the pier would deprive Venice of its economic lifeblood." The Council referred the recommendation to the Parks and Recreation Department. Naturally they refused to grant an extension since officials had been adamantly against Venice's honky-tonk atmosphere since the day they annexed the city.

It was a sad day, the end of an era, when the pier closed at midnight on Saturday April 20, 1946.

The Venice Pier closed at midnight April 20, 1946.

Aerial view of demolition operations of the Venice Pier in spring 1947. The pier wreckage had not burned prior to this photograph.

Attractions that thrilled millions like the Fun House, Giant Dipper roller coaster, the Great American Racing Derby, Niagara Barrel, Flying Circus, Scooter and Dragon Bamboo Slide would be dismantled and sold if possible. Amusement men, who were both sad and angry, had no idea where they would go.

The Kinney Company and its concessionaires had until May 15th to remove anything salvageable. The Racing Derby was dismantled and sold to Ocean Beach in San Francisco and the Flying Circus was sold for scrap. Rudy Illions sent his right hand man, John Payne, to pack up the Scooter ride. It was headed for Long Beach. The crew removed the cars first, then loaded the sections of heavy steel plate flooring onto their truck. They were about ready to drive off when the terrible sound of groaning, cracking wood, alerted them to jump clear of the truck. The pier's rotted decking suddenly gave way and the heavy loaded truck plunged through the jagged hole to the surf below. They eventually recovered the truck and its load.

Dismantlement of the remainder of the buildings, pier decking and unsalvagable rides would continue for nearly a year. Workers reported finding thousands of buttons and coins when they tore up the subfloorings of the rides. Finally, in May 1947, arson finished the job. Boys set fire to the framework of the Bamboo Slide and flames quickly spread to the roller coaster, the only other remaining structure.

The Kinney Company confidently made plans for a new amusement park to be located elsewhere, but they were financially strapped. Charles Lorman instead announced plans in May 1947 for a $2.5 million park on a 70 acre tract at Dell Avenue and Washington Street. His Ocean View Amusement Park would include the 17 acre Lake Los Angeles to be developed as an aquatic sports center. The park would have an elaborate midway, roller coaster, merry-go-round, children's rides, bowling alleys and a skating rink. A shortage of building materials prevented them from immediately starting construction. Lorman was soon replaced by Earle Charleton who scaled down the project significantly.

Ocean Front Walk was nearly deserted after the pier closed. Only a few buildings remain on the beach side of the street, 1949. (above)

St. Marks Hotel is connected to its annex across Speedway by the Bridge of Sighs, 1949. (right)

Eventually John Lorman and Herbert Schmeck developed Hoppyland on the site in 1949. They convinced William Boyd, also known as Hoppalong Cassidy, to lend his name to the small 22 ride kiddie park. It featured a 35 foot high Philadelphia Toboggan Company Junior roller coaster called the Little Dipper, a small double ferris wheel, a Rapids ride, an Allen Herschel carnival style merry-go-round, pony rides and several small flat spinning rides like the Whirlwind. One kiddie ride had hand cranked cars that travelled on railroad tracks. The big entertainment attraction was the Globe of Death where a motorcycle rider rode around on the inside of a wire cage. The park wasn't profitable and only lasted four seasons.

The beach widening project begun in 1947 resulted in the sluicing of over 14 million tons of sand from the dune site of the proposed Hyperion Sewage Treatment Plant in El Segundo to as far north as the Ocean Park Pier. The width of the beach along the eight mile stretch was increased to a uniform 500 feet. By the summer of 1948 sluicing progressed as far as Brooks Avenue. It was strange to see the Sunset Pier completely landlocked, the beach stretching far beyond its outer pilings. The project, including the sewage plant, was completed in 1950. The beach quarantine was lifted the following year.

Fortunately the Ocean Park Pier entered a period of renovation just after World War II and kept the area's amusement park tradition alive. First they installed a double ferris wheel near the end of the pier. Edmund Martine's huge Strat-o-liner ride was also nearing completion. He and chief designer Bob Goldsworthy had started working on it in 1941 but the war had interrupted their endeavor. When its four large sleek cars were finally attached to the tower's long swivel arms in 1946, pier people predicted the cars would fly off and land in the ocean.

The Chute the Chutes closed permanently in late summer after an accident claimed the life of a little boy. He stood up and fell out of the boat as it slid down the ramp. Four years later Harry Cooper's Kiddy Town opened at the bottom of the ramp where the pool stood. This enclosed area had a miniature roller coaster, an airplane ride and several small kiddie car rides.

But even these changes did little to increase business or the waning popularity of the old-fashioned amusement pier. Teenagers and young adults with families were indoors watching television or driving their cars to outdoor movie theaters for entertainment. Also, the closing of the bingo games in 1949 deprived the pier,

especially the Lick Pier side, of much of its income. Pacific Electric's decision to shut down 'red car' service to the Venice / Ocean Park area on September 15, 1970 didn't help either.

By 1951 Lick Pier's Aragon Ballroom had fallen on hard times. The most recent orchestra to play there only drew eight couples, and KTLA television dropped its weekly telecasts. Its manager, Gordon "Pops' Sadrup, in one last effort to salvage his declining dance business, hired band leader Lawrence Welk to perform a miracle. Welk's brand of light popular danceable music had drawn crowds at the Aragon back in 1946 despite the competition of Tommy Dorsey at the nearby Casino Gardens.

Welk played at the Aragon and KTLA was persuaded to resume the telecasts. His first televised show on May 2, 1951 drew numerous viewers despite the late midnight hour. Before long the Dodge dealers of Southern California became sponsors, and Welk's "Champagne music", live from the Aragon Ballroom, became a popular national television show.

The Venice area continued to deteriorate physically throughout the fifties. Pawnshops and liquor stores replaced the souvenir shops and bingo parlors. Tourists were replaced by derelicts, drug addicts and motorcycle gangs, and winos passed out laid beneath the sheltered colonnaded archways on Windward Avenue. Property values, far from rising, dropped dramatically.

On June 23, 1957, the Urban Renewal Agency in Los Angeles announced that a portion of the city's $100 million in federally allocated funds would be available for redevelopment in the Venice area. Karl Ouiston, assistant coordinator of the agency suggested a survey to determine the feasibility of urban redevelopment in the community. He formed the Venice Urban Renewal Advisory Committee to sample local opinion. The majority of Venice's property owners were against relinquishing title to their property. In March 1958 they voted against the urban redevelopment survey and Ouiston cancelled it.

In the late fifties a new group of people began to settle in the Venice area. They adopted a new lifestyle that rejected the bland contemporary values of work and success in favor of a Bohemian life centered on poetry, jazz and art. Jack Kerouac's novel called them the 'Beat Generation'.

The Beats were lured by Venice's low rent, mild climate and toleration of their lifestyle. They included painters like John Altoon, Ben Talbert, Tony Landreau, George Herms and Fowad Magdalani — "the mad artist of

Venice West" who experimented with the limits of abstraction and new forms of assemblage works. Their work was a pallid imitation of New York's 10th Street abstract expressionism. The poets included Stuart Perkoff, Frank Rios, Tony Scibella, Lawrence Lipton, and James Ryan Morris. They wrote about disenchantment and nuclear overkill. Others included folksinger Julie Meredith, light show impresario Jimmy Alonzi and sculptor Tati.

Coffee houses like the Gas House and Venice West were the hubs of their world. They were gathering places for the artists and poets who often sat at tables either alone writing or with others in deep philosophical conversation or in deep concentration playing chess. The owners decorated the walls with the group's paintings and works of art. In the evenings they held poetry readings, and scheduled jazz combos or folk singing as entertainment.

Lawrence Lipton chronicled the coffee houses, personal searches, artists, poets and others of "Venice West" in his book 'The Holy Barbarians'. He called Venice the 'slum-by-the-sea'. The book's publicity brought thousands of the curious to the Venice scene, and too many of them hung on. Weekend tourists who came to gawk drove many of the artists underground. Eventually a hostile 'anti-Beat' reaction began among the local civic groups.

The Gas House and its owner "Big Daddy" Nord became the center of controversy. It needed an entertainment license from the Los Angeles Police Commission if it was to continue its programs of jazz and poetry. The Venice Civic Union, vowing to end Bohemianism in Venice, campaigned to have the request denied. The Beats armed themselves with a petition urging that the license be granted, but the commission denied their request.

Civic pressure on the Gas House continued. The fire department issued citations for over-crowding and the police fined them for charging parking fees without a permit. They were often struck by vandalism, police vice raids and drug arrests. Finally they closed their doors in 1960.

The Venice West Cafe on Dudley Avenue lasted longer. Its founder John Kenevan was eventually joined by John and Anna Haag who came to Venice to write poetry. But as the 60's wore on and the "Beat Scene", with its disciples either dead, jailed or scattered to other scenes, began to slowly disintegrate, it too closed its doors in 1966. It wouldn't, however, spell the end of the counter-culture revolution, for the Beats were soon

Felix the Cat game concession on the Ocean Park Pier.

followed by a new generation of "flower children".

The end of the 'Beat' era didn't necessarily mean the end of the innovative art in Venice. Many art-educated upcoming artists gravitated to Venice in the early 60's because studio space was cheap. The first wave, who settled along Market and Main streets, included Peter Alexander, Billy Al Bengston, Ron Cooper, John Altoon and Dewain Valentine. They were soon joined in the late 60's by Chuck Arnoldi, Laddie Dill, Ann McCoy, Tom Wudi and Tony Berlant. It is sad, but as Venice became more important as a creative community, it became increasingly more difficult for struggling artists to live there.

In 1961 a new effort was made at revitalizing the community and checking its decay. Los Angeles City Councilman Karl Rundberg formed the Venice Planning Committee composed of representatives of fourteen separate civic organizations. They requested that Los Angeles implement a program of building code enforcement of existing housing and safety regulations in an area bounded by Ocean Front Walk (west), Main Street (east), Brooks Avenue (north) and 18th Avenue (south). Essentially they wanted city building inspectors to force property owners to improve their structures.

The city agreed to the request. Owners would either have the make the necessary repairs to their buildings or demolish them at their own expense. Those that didn't comply would be subject to legal action. If the pilot phase was successful, the program would be expanded in three stages. The whole project would take three and one half years.

Inspection of the first two buildings began in January 1962. Both the Gas House and the St. Marks Hotel failed to pass code. The city judged them to be in such a state of deterioration that repairing them would be useless. They were condemned and ordered to be demolished. The owners demanded a public hearing.

After nearly every building on Windward Avenue was either condemned or the owners were asked to make extensive repairs, property owners formed an organization called the Shoreline & Landmarks Society. It was headed by Mrs. Eleanor Lally, manager of the St. Marks, and Harvey Sawyer, owner of a commercial building on Windward. Their goal was to have the Cultural Heritage Board declare the Venetian style buildings replicas of those in Venice, Italy and have them preserved for historical value. The Board said the buildings weren't representative of Southern California architecture and denied them landmark status.

View of the main midway on the Ocean Park Pier; 1950.

Skooter ride on the Ocean Park Pier; 1952. (above)

Looff carousel on the Ocean Park Pier; 1952. (above)

The society hired a lawyer to represent them in their fight against code enforcement. On July 30, 1962 their lawyer, Phil Silver, filed a suit in Los Angeles Superior court asking for a moratorium. The suit's main point was that the city had no legal right to apply present building standards on structures constructed before the present standards went into effect, unless those structures were a menace to life, limb, health or property. They lost.

The building department advised the property owners on Windward's north side that they could, if they like, at considerable expense remove their unsafe upper floors. Demolition of all but two of the structures was begun by June 1965. The St Charles was brought up to present building standards, and the owners of the Windward Hotel fought demolition in court. They ended up removing a portion of the upper floors in their building.

Phase II and III of the inspections took place in 1963 and 1964 with little opposition. By the end of 1965, 550 buildings, one third of the Venice community was demolished. The rest were repaired and brought up to building code. It was supposed to be for the better, but Venice took on the appearance of a bombed out war zone, just cleared of rubble.

Property owners along the south Venice canals, inspired by the recently finished Marina del Rey harbor, envisioned grandiose plans for their area. The Venice Canals Improvement Association, started by Henry Greene and Barbara Jean Hayes, proposed widening and dredging the canals to an 11 foot high-tide depth. The canals were to be lined with concrete and connected with the new harbor. A high concrete bridge would span the canals at Washington Street.

They presented a petition to the city representing 80% of the canal property owners. Their estimate for the project of $3.85 million soon spiraled upward once the city became involved. By 1965 when bids were sought, the Board of Public Works expected them to come in just under $17 million. Unfortunately, none of the 70 firms that inspected the plans offered to bid on the project.

Meanwhile opposition to the project began to mount, especially from property owners who owned no canal frontage and felt that they shouldn't be assessed. The surrounding property owners were dropped from the assessment and tenants of the area's run down housing were offered relocation expenses should they need it.

In 1971 legal complications delayed the project. The Hughes Tool Company, owner of 34 lots within the project boundaries filed suit against the project. They claimed that the expenditure of funds for relocation was illegal. Then a month later the Western Center for Law and Poverty filed suit on the tenant's behalf. They claimed that the project would "produce a community in which only the wealthy would be able to live." The canal residents, mostly tenants, staged annual canal festivals to publicize their case.

The law suits were consolidated and eventually were heard in court. In 1973 Superior Court Judge Jerry Pacht ruled that the city had to prepare an environmental impact report on the canal project before proceeding. As usual local politics had delayed a project until it was no longer economically feasible. The city council with no recourse voted to abandon the project.

In the early 60's the city, using money from bond issues passed in the late 50's, built a new recreation center along the beach. The old Venice Pier site had been purchased in 1950 from the Abbot Kinney Company for $640,000. Athletic facilities, beach parking and a main pavilion building were constructed and opened in 1962. There were plans to construct a swimming pool beside the pavilion, but when costs escalated and the Board of Education offered to contribute, the location was shifted inland adjacent to the Venice High School campus.

The city had high hopes for the pavilion, but plans for live theatrical performances died when the promoter declared bankruptcy. Also, cold ocean breezes restricted the use of the open air facility to warm summer nights. They thought that adding a roof at a cost of $221,000 in 1969 would fix things, but the covering created unforseen acoustical problems.

Venice in the 70's was marked by slow growth. Political groups like the Venice Town Council with the help of the newly created California Coastal Commission managed to mount opposition against any project that would alter the character of the community. They felt that the poor had just as much right to live in the community as the rich people that were buying property to develop. They realized that a dramatic increase in property values was on a collision course with the community's entrenched low-income population. Increasing numbers of poor were being forced out of the community they had lived in for decades. The Town Council's goal was to delay, or at least scale down, any projects that would radically effect surrounding property values and the rents charged to its tenants. They seemed to prefer empty ugly lots, parking lots if need be, anything but upscale development. What they didn't foresee or count on was Venice's rebirth as a major tourist destination.

Windward Avenue looking west from Pacific Avenue; 1955.

CHAPTER 8

Pacific Ocean Park
(1958-1967)

In 1956 CBS and the Los Angeles Turf Club were granted the lease on the Ocean Park Pier and they proposed to build a $10,000,000 nautical theme park to compete with Disneyland. They closed the pier after Labor Day, hired the best amusement park designers and Hollywood special effects experts they could find and began to design innovative new attractions for the theme park. In all 80 special effects men, scenic designers and artists worked for more than a year on the project. They like Disney, found corporate sponsors to share the expenses of some of the exhibits. To save money they renovated existing buildings and incorporated six of the old attractions into the layout; the merry-go-round, roller coaster, Tonnerville Fun House, Glass House, twin diving bells and Strat-o-liner ride. They called the new park Pacific Ocean Park.

The 28 acre park was decorated throughout in a sea-green and white art moderne look, an evocation of the ocean itself. Its entrance set amidst fountains, sculptures and large sea horse and clam shell decorated frieze, set the mood of the wonders within. The ticket booth in Neptune's Courtyard was set under a six legged concrete starfish canopy; plastic bubbles and seahorses adorned its top. All day admission was ninety cents for adults, less for children. This included access to the park, Neptune's Kingdom, the Sea Circus and Westinghouse Enchanted Forest exhibit. Other rides and attractions were at additional costs.

Opening day on Saturday July 28, 1958 drew 20,000 curious people and dozens of Hollywood celebrities. Sunday's 37,262 paying customers brought traffic jams to the area. During its first six days it out performed Disneyland in attracting customers.

Visitors entered the park through Neptune's Kingdom where they took a submarine elevator down to the suboceanic corridors below. Water filling the elevator's clear central tube gave the illusion of descending beneath the sea. Across from the elevator was an enormous sea tank set in the corridor wall. It was partitioned so that it appeared that shark and prey cohabited the same tank. Beyond and covering one entire wall along the corridor was a large diorama filled

Neptune's Courtyard entrance to Pacific Ocean Park.

Pacific Ocean Park — 1959

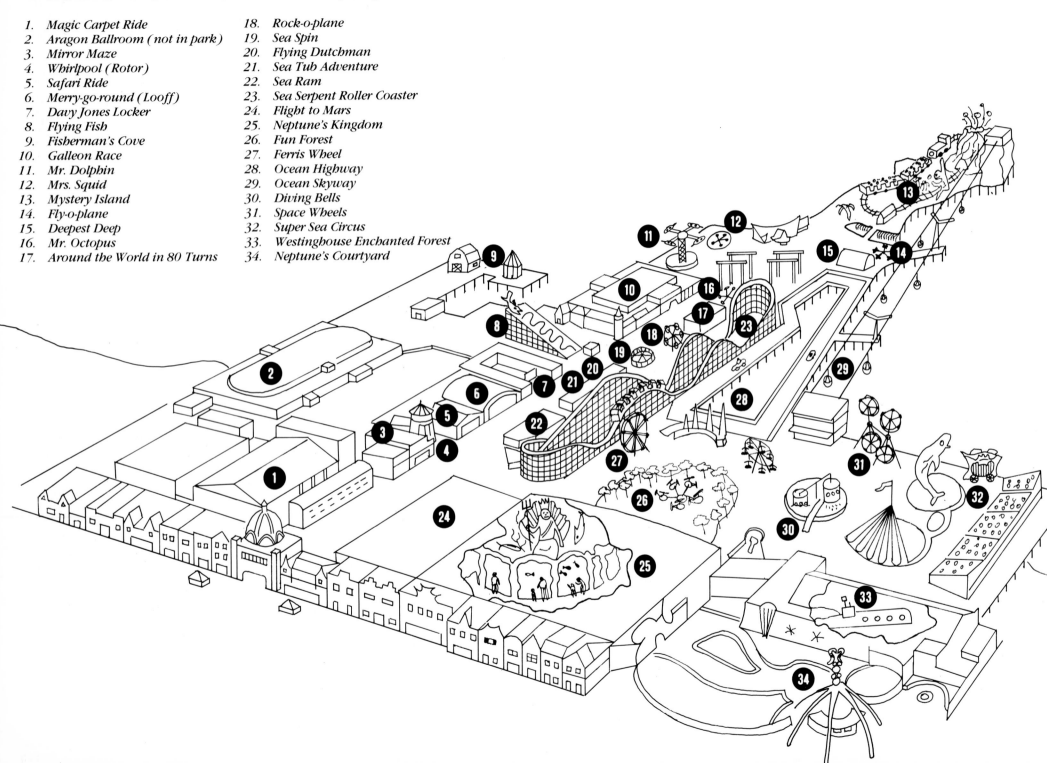

Aerial view of Pacific Ocean Park; 1963.

Ocean Skyway bubble cars travelled from the area near the entrance out to Mystery Island and back.

with creatures that couldn't live in captivity. Motorized artificial turtles, manta rays, sawfish, and sharks glided by over coral reef and hanging seaweed. In the distance, barely visible in the glimmering light was Neptune with his septor in hand sitting on his throne. The display was a masterpiece of special effects, a convincing illusion of waterless liquid space presented by your Coca Cola bottler.

Next door was Westinghouse's free Enchanted Forest and Nautilus Submarine exhibit. They had a 150 foot model, atomic reactor section of the famous atomic sub. Nearby was a room full of electronic appliances and gadgets for the House of Tomorrow. A modular house was put together by machinery as part of the show.

The main feature of the Sea Circus area was the performing seal and dolphin shows. Two thousand people could watch the shows several times daily in the large amphitheater. Afterwards they could feed the seals in the Seal Pool.

The twin Diving Bells nearby offered excursions beneath the surface of a large salt water tank. As one of the bells was loaded with passengers, the other was slowly pulled below the surface by hydraulic pistons. Those inside peered out of the small portholes in search of fish. Water seeping through the bell's riveted metal seams reminded one of the tremendous pressure outside. Then there was a sudden rush upwards, and the ride was over as the diving bell popped explosively to the surface. The two long lines of people, nervously awaiting their turn, were splashed by the sudden surge of water.

The Ocean Skyway entrance was but a few steps away. Here passengers could board bubble gondolas for a six minute, half mile ride that would take them 75 feet above the Pacific. It offered panoramic views of the bay, Santa Monica Mountains, and the park. As it reached its turn-around point near the Mystery Island's volcanic peak, it offered a tantalizing preview of the Banana Train ride.

Union 76's miniature Ocean Highway gave drivers a choice of futuristic styled model cars. The long, nearly oval course was build like a causeway directly over the ocean. Other rides in that section of the park included a ferris wheel and a tilted aerial style ride called the Paratrooper. Its two passenger seats suspended from parachute canopies swung outwards as the ride gained speed.

On the other side of Neptune's Kingdom was a unique attraction called Flight to Mars. The inside lobby was decorated with a mural featuring a barren Martian

A local beauty queen poses beside King Neptune

landscape. Space travellers entered a round tiered spaceship-like theater with a column bank of television screens set in the floor's center. The doors sealed and the seats reclined back as the ship prepared for flight. The whole theater and the individual seats shook during takeoff, while views of Earth receding in the distance were projected on the television monitors. A few minutes later the ship approached Mars and passengers prepared for a landing and were made to feel like they were slowly descending. The whole theater was build like an elevator so when passengers exited they stood before vast dioramas of the red planet and its green alien creatures. Visitors were magically returned to Earth by entering a mirrored black light teleport chamber at the exit door.

Across the main midway was the Flying Carpet ride, a fantasy excursion into the 'Tales of the Arabian Nights'. Passengers boarded vehicles resembling large flying carpets that were suspended from above on tracks. The cars soared high into the air above the city lights below, past lofty mountains painted on the walls, and far away to the Sinbad's Bagdad where Arabian palace spires soared skyward. Below was a giant genie coming out of Ali Baba's lamp, and other characters from the old tales and legends. To attract customers they hired a giant 7′ 4″ tall man whose Arabian Nights costume and large turban made him look gigantic.

The Mirror Maze in the next building was a standard Fun House style attraction. The building's transparent facade revealed dozens of reflected images of each of the people inside the labyrinth. One had to first find a path through a glass maze to get to the area where the floors moved. Barrels turned, and rooms slanted, daring one to stand up straight. Then it was back into another maze of glass and mirrors to find a way out.

Davy Jones Locker further along the midway was a much more interesting Fun House with a nautical theme. The revamped Tonnerville Fun House was a walk thru with tunnels decorated with fake underwater paraphernalia including divers in old helmets. It had a crooked room, two slides with a bump in the center and dozens of distorted mirrors. Customers had to squeeze through giant upright padded rollers to exit. Teenagers liked the attraction because it was mostly dark inside.

Almost across from it was the Flying Dutchman, a 'dark' ride on tracks. Treasure chest styled cars passed through the hull of an old Spanish galleon where it narrowly missed upsetting a stack of rum barrels. Inside behind bars were prisoners crying to get out, and further on skeletons of those who were imprisoned far

Union 76's miniature Ocean Highway. (opposite page)   *Pacific Ocean Park's main midway featured numerous thrill rides. (above)*

too long. Threatening pirates gathered in one cabin to argue over their treasure. The overflowing treasure chest nearby had gold doubloons and jewels spilling out.

The Deepest Deep was a smaller 'dark' ride that gave the illusion of exploring the sea in a two-man submersible. People would ride in a tracked car with a plastic bubble dome past fake looking underwater scenes. A hydraulic piston raised, lowered and turned the cars as they passed different scenes like mermaids and treasure chests. The ride was cheaply done and had endless mechanical problems that kept it closed much of the time.

Round the World in 80 Turns took one for a tour of France, England, Germany, Turkey, China and Japan. The tub-like cars would whip sharply to the left or right to change scenes. Due to constant complaints of nausea and neck pains it was closed midway through the second season.

Fun seekers could try hunting for big game on the Safari Ride. Tracked jeeps equipped with electronic rifles wound its way through African jungle. Lion prides fought over a recent kill and an occasional Rhino would charge the jeep. The man-made plywood cutout animals were slightly animated.

There were plenty of old fashioned thrill rides along the Ports O' POP midway. Foremost was the Sea Serpent roller coaster. It was from the old pier but was now painted in an array of gaudy colors. The Whirl Pool was a huge centrifuge that pinned customers to the wall, then the floor dropped out. Another centrifuge ride called the Shell Spin slowly tilted until riders were being spun vertically. The old Strat-o-liner ride was now called Mr. Dolphin, and the Flying Fish was merely a 'wild mouse' coaster with cars decorated to look like fish. Nearby were Octopus and Mrs. Squid rides. The latter was a flat 'Scrambler' style ride whose cars would swing back and forth across the platform. They spun and appeared to narrowly miss each other as they crossed each other.

The park's best ride was the Mystery Island Banana Train Ride at the end of the pier. Eight giant totem poles and two outrigger canoes formed the entrance to the area. Explorers crossed a suspension bridge above a 9000 gallon per minute waterfall to an authentic Polynesian stilt house where they boarded the U.S. Rubber train. The train, like those of tropical banana plantation trains, was pushed by the locomotive.

The excursion carried one through a tropical paradise of palms, bamboo, and banana trees, past coconut throwing monkeys and into two back to back counter-

Twin diving bells took visitors beneath the sea. (opposite page)   *Space Wheels ride consisted of twin double Ferris wheels.*

Davy Jones Locker had typical fun house mirrors that bent and distorted one's image.

The Sea Serpent roller coaster was the most exciting thrill ride in the park.
(opposite page)

The Safari ride gave kids a chance to hunt wild animals.

The Sea Tub Adventure ride was the park's 'Tunnel of Love'.

View looking east of Pacific Ocean Park's main midway.

The Whirl Pool was the classic rotor ride where the floor dropped out. (above)

Shell Spin ride. (left)

rotating tunnels that simulated an earthquake. The tunnels led to inside the heart of an erupting volcano where the train circled the bubbling volcanic crater. Once the passengers passed through the spider caves, the train's precarious tracks suddenly emerged on a suspension bridge over real ocean surf below. Before the startled passengers realized it, the train just as suddenly reentered the mountain into a large room where geysers erupted. Finally it passed through a tropical rain storm complete with lightning and through the jungle to the passenger loading station. Then as the ride came to an end a friendly gooney bird shrieked, "Hope you enjoyed your trip!"

The park had two dining and shopping areas. Inside the park was a recreation of a New England harbor called Fisherman's Cove. Outside along Ocean Front Walk was the International Promenade offering superb cuisine in authentic foreign restaurants, as well as exotic souvenirs, gifts and imports in the various shops.

Apparently many people enjoyed Pacific Ocean Park, for by the time it closed for construction and remodeling on January 5, 1959, it had attracted 1,190,000 visitors. Management decided to add four new attractions at a cost of nearly $2,000,000.

Fun Forest located near the Sea Circus was primarily for children. It had helicopter, boat and covered wagon rides. It also had a picturesque tree maze with slides and other surprises. They purchased a 96 passenger ride called Space Wheels for $225,000 and placed it between the whale tank and Ocean Skyway ride. It was comprised of four ferris wheels, stacked two high, which rotated at the ends of our giant arms. Each wheel in turn spun in its own orbit as the arms revolved.

The company planned to add an ornate bandstand area for entertainment and 8700 square feet of space on the south end of the pier for Zooland. This area adjacent to Fisherman's Cove would feature baby polar bears, penguins, otters, flamingos, and other aquatic animals. Neither of these two attractions were completed.

The second season's attendance wasn't nearly as good as the first. The owners decided to close it in October for the winter, then announced a month later that they sold the park to John Morehard for $10,000,000.

It was obvious to the new owner that the park needed a one price admission policy to attract more customers. He set a price for the following spring of $1.50 for adults and $1.00 for children. He did, however, expect to raise prices for the busy summer tourist season. The Sea Serpent roller coaster was still an extra twenty five cents per ride since it was the one ride not owned by the park.

Mr. Dolphin aerial ride.

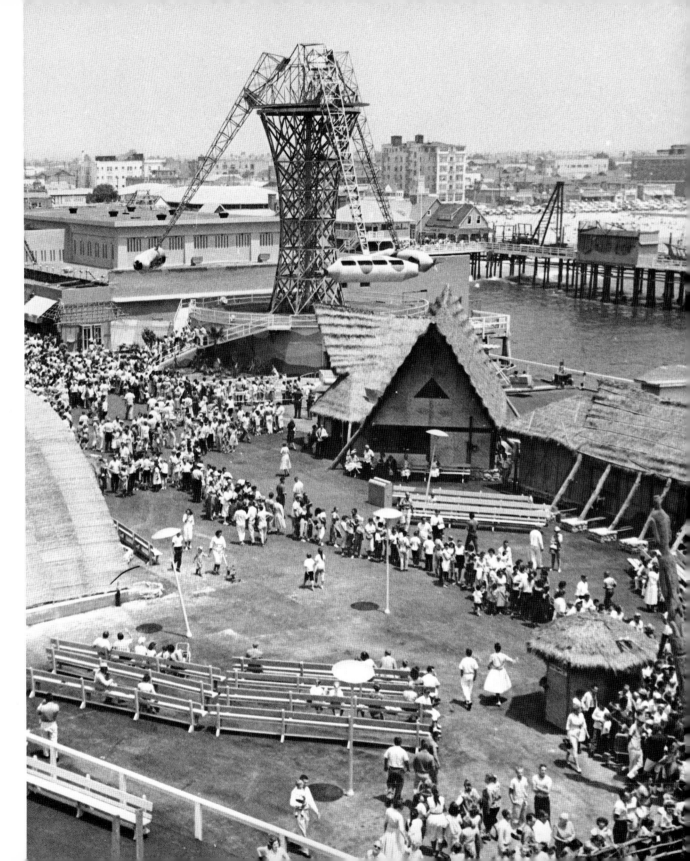

Entrance to Mystery Island was across a suspension bridge.

View of Mystery Island.

Banana train travels through a tropical paradise at the beginning of the Mystery Island ride.

The Banana train's precarious tracks exit a tunnel and cross a bridge directly over the ocean far below.

Morehard's goal was to run the park as a small family amusement park business not as competition to Disneyland. He hoped to attract teens and family repeat business from people who lived within 30 to 40 miles.

Unfortunately the park continued to lose customers. The trouble was that Pacific Ocean Park was in a run down, seedy part of town and the area attracted the wrong element. The nearby streets were littered with bums and winos who accosted customers for money. Local teenagers, aware that their parents frowned on them going to the park on weekend evenings, often told them they were going to a movie and then sneaked down to P.O.P.

Local kids had a knack for sneaking into the park for nothing. They often used a catwalk beneath the pier to reach a trapdoor near the shooting gallery. Sometimes it was unlocked, but if that failed they would climb over the high exit turnstile.

The park, too, was having trouble maintaining its own operation. It offered a large number of rides and attractions for the price, but with such a high overhead it had to skimp on maintenance. Rides were often broken and everything deteriorated against the rough ocean elements. In short, the park with its peeling paint looked run down. It did, however, attract 1,216,000 paid customers in 1963.

It was sold in October 1963 to Irving Kay, a San Francisco real estate developer for $7.5 million. The deal included some other property. At first he leased P.O.P. back to management headed by Jack Roberts, but then in January he sold the park to Robert's company, Amusement Purchase, Inc. for $2.5 million.

The 1964 season was the park's most successful, attendance wise. It drew 1,663,013 visitors. New rides included a flat ride called the Himalaya near the Sea Circus, and a Monster Mouse steel rollercoaster where Fun Forest stood. The coaster's ability to make abrupt 90 degree turns made the ride downright frightening. Passengers thought that the cars had jumped the track as the front of its small cars hung over the narrow track edge before they abruptly turned. The smaller Flying Fish 'wild mouse' was replaced by a small Ferris Wheel and tilted centrifuge called the Mixer that were located elsewhere in the park, and the kiddie rides were moved to the Fisherman's Village area.

But Santa Monica in 1965 began its Ocean Park urban renewal project. There was wholesale demolition of nearby buildings and closings of streets leading to the park. The entire area was disordered while they were building two large apartment towers. A street leading to

Mystery Island has geysers, erupting volcanos, earthquakes and tropical storms.

Rock-O-Plane ride on the main midway.

Mr. Octopus ride.

ENTRANCE

Flying Dutchman ride was a 'dark ride' inside a pirate's galleon. (left)

The Flying Fish ride was a small steel 'wild mouse' coaster. (below)

Front of the Westinghouse Enchanted Forest exhibit.

Union 76's Ocean Highway and Ocean Skyway loading station.

Paratrooper ride.

Twin Diving Bells.

Sea Circus Seal Show.

the park would be open one week, then deliberately closed the next. Customers often called from nearby phone booths to complain that they could see the park but couldn't figure out how to get there. Attendance dropped to 621,000 in 1965 and 398,700 in 1966. Roberts paid bills rarely, not even his modest lease rent to Santa Monica.

Santa Monica was ready to pull his park license at a meeting on March 16, 1967 when Roberts showed up at the last minute with a fistfull of policies proving that the park was covered with $1.5 million in insurance. The city was ready to close the park when they got a cancellation notice from his insurance company.

The Urban Redevelopment board was concerned that his park with its peeling paint and boarded up restaurants along Ocean Front Walk would scare away prospective apartment tenants. Although they would have liked to see the park closed, and nearly accomplished it during construction, they publicly wished Roberts well.

Roberts, despite years of lagging attendance and piles of long overdue bills, expected things to improve. He was negotiating a loan of $1,600,000 from the Teamsters. In addition, urban redevelopment left him with a brand new access street, ample parking and a bus stop. The Cheetah, a mod rock and roll club planned to open in the Aragon Ballroom.

Finally at the end of the 1967 season, P.O.P.'s creditors took action and forced the park into involuntary bankruptcy. Santa Monica precipitated the action when they filed a suit to take control of the property because Roberts owed them $17,000 in back rent since 1965. The park closed on October 6, 1967.

A.J. Bumb became Trustee of the park, and on April 25, 1968 federal bankruptcy referee Norman Neukom gave permission to dispose of the park. When he was asked if P.O.P. might be saved, he replied "No Chance! Santa Monica doesn't want it there".

The auction began on June 28, 1968 and ran through the 30th. The proceeds from the sale of 36 rides and sixteen games were used to pay off creditors. The park's dilapidated buildings and pier structure remained until several fires and the final demolition in the winter 1973-1974 removed it from all but people's fond memories. The long era of Venice / Ocean Park amusement parks was finally over.

Entrance to Mystery Island.

CHAPTER 9

Ocean Front Walk - An Unstructured Midway
(1972 —)

Harry Parry, street entertainer; 1982. (above)
Steve McPeak performs without a net on a tightrope strung between two buildings across Windward Avenue; 1978.
Ocean Front Walk in front of the Sidewalk Cafe at Horizon Street; 1979. (right)

Venice's Ocean Front Walk was a relatively empty and quiet place in 1972. The wide walkway was frequented mostly by lower middle class families that lived along the side streets, elderly Jews living on pensions in ocean front hotels, down on their luck winos looking for a handout, and free spirits of all ages and nationalities who wanted nothing more than a day at the beach. Several grocery stores, a bakery and a restaurant or two satisfied the needs of the residents. The area looked run down with boarded up buildings and vacant lots. There were very few tourists because there was nothing to see unless one was a sociology or urban planning student.

That spring the city constructed a bicycle path adjacent to Ocean Front Walk. It was part of the county's bicycle route that extended 18 miles along the ocean from Torrance Beach to Santa Monica. The route exposed Venice to thousands of bicycle riders who would have otherwise avoided the seedy looking area.

Sometimes bicyclists would stop at Venice's recreation center to watch weightlifters work out at "Muscle Beach" an outdoor weight pen. Well known weightlifters like Arnold Schwarzeneggar could occasionally be seen working out there. Behind it was a sand covered area full of gymnastic equipment. The center also had eight paddle tennis courts, four handball courts and two basketball courts.

A few entertainers played to passers-by along Ocean Front Walk at the north end of Venice on weekends. One of the first, a ragtime piano player, rolled out his piano and placed it adjacent to the bicycle path. A crowd would gather and sometimes a long-haired flutist who lived nearby would join in. Nearby was a bearded young man blowing huge bubbles, who would fascinate children and their parents as he walked along the oceanfront. The sound of drums beating could often be heard in the distance. Black bongo players occupied one of the green roofed pagodas along the boardwalk at Westminster.

In the summer of 1974 nude sunbathing brought more attention to Venice than the town rightly deserved or even desired. Bathing 'au natural' was something Venice's free spirts considered perfectly normal. But once the media reported the phenomenon, Venice was completely unprepared for the onslaught of weird, sexually-repressed Americans looking for Venice's Nude Beach. Gay exhibitionists, pornographic photographers and leering voyeurs came by the carload. It was a freak show patrolled by the LAPD Beach Patrol trying to blend in by wearing blue shorts and white T shirt uniforms.

The newly created but non-elected Venice Town Council, champion of everyone's rights, felt that after the novelty wore off everything would return to normal. They voted unanimously for the freedom of individual choice and to keep the beach open for nude or clad sunbathing. The Los Angeles City Council saw it differently. They voted 14 to 1 for a cover-up. But it was too late to turn back the clock for people had discovered that Venice still existed and was actually a relatively safe place to visit during the day.

Tom Sewell and Rodger Webster were some of the first people who saw commercial potential in recycling the area's old buildings. They bought an old laundromat in 1973 at Windward and Pacific and transformed it into four boutiques and restaurants. Latter they bought other run down buildings on Windward and remodeled them.

Robert and Mary Goodfader bought an empty, 50 year old boarded up brick building on Ocean Front Walk that stood across from the old Venice Plunge. In 1976 they transformed it into a bookstore and 40 table sidewalk cafe that soon became a popular local hangout for the artists and writers in the area.

Goodfader also gained the leases on two large vacant oceanfront lots on both corners of Windward. Vendors mostly local artists, and a few who sold ragtag junk and old clothing rented space for $40 a month. The remainder of the space was used for beach parking.

Early in 1977 Jeff Rosenberg leased a space from Goodfader and began renting rollerskates out the back of his van. He called his operation Cheapskates. It rented skates with innovative polyurethane wheels that allowed skaters to glide easily over rough concrete and asphalt surfaces. Venice's wide Ocean Front Walk and smooth bicycle path made it the perfect outdoor roller rink and it soon became a popular spot to try the outdoor sport.

By spring 1978 the skate rental business had become so successful that competitors appeared. Suzanne Thomas and Phil Lacey moved their small skate rental stand from the Park Avenue lot to the Windward lot across from Cheapskates. When two other small rental stands also leased space in Goodfader's lots, Cheapskates decided to move into a storefront on Ocean Front Walk between Westminster and Clubhouse where they had space to expand their rental and sales operation. Thomas and Lacy got their break during the summer when a seedy pawnshop vacated a storefront on Windward. They moved Venice Precision Rollerworks there. It was excellent timing and a perfect location, for

when the media began publicizing the new fad, they had the space to expand. Their 250 pair rental operation was soon grossing $6000-8000 per week.

Outdoor rollerskating began to attract people from all walks of life, all economic strata. It wasn't unusual to see a group of matronly ladies park their Mercedes in a beach lot and ask the attendant for directions to one of the skate rental shops. Soon there were thousands of skaters sharing Ocean Front Walk with pedestrians. The local youth set up tin cans in front of the pavilion and used the wide approach as a slalom course. Others jumped a row of five or six trash cans laid flat for sport. A disco skating area was set up nearby and it attracted large crowds of black inner-city youth. Mayor Bradley in a gesture of largess declared, "Venice is the roller skating capital of the world."

The owners of Venice Precision Rollerworks now with a third partner, Ron Walden, had more ambitious plans. First they added a retail sales outlet called Roadskates a half block away on Windward, and a asphalt roller rink on an empty L shaped lot behind and beside their rental store on Windward. Then they embarked on a franchising system throughout California and Europe.

Unfortunately the roller skating fad peaked at the end of 1979 and was dying by the end of 1980. Roadskates had expanded too fast, was financially overextended, and its owners had spent lavishly on promotion and a fast life style. In early 1981 the merchandise in the company's warehouse was secretly moved during the night and the owners vanished, possibly to Europe. They left creditors with bills totalling in excess of one half million dollars.

Their failure and the subsequent closing of numerous rollerskating businesses that had dotted many locations along the Ocean Front Walk did little to dampen the public's new found enthusiasm for Venice. Venice got a boost from extensive world wide publicity, and tourists swarmed Ocean Front Walk on weekends and even throughout the week during the peak summer season. The boardwalk had become the perfect place to people watch. People felt free to dress and act uninhibited, whether it was punk style green and pink hair or dressed in scanty bathing attire that showed off their well developed bodies. Black guys would call "Hey beautiful" when a blond-haired woman with a shapely body passed. It was a multi-racial place where it wasn't unusual to see a black man a blond haired woman together. The only people who looked out of place were the few that wore business suits.

The noise was always loud and pervasive. People could ignore the fire and brimstone preachers, but the distorted sound from sixty pound 'ghettoblasters' that inner city youth carried only hurt the ears. Visitors were so distracted that few noticed those taking their eight foot long pythons, ugly green chameleons or babbling parrots for a walk unless a crowd gathered. Many called the boardwalk a circus but in a matter of speaking it was an unstructured midway. When it was packed it was a zoo.

Its reputation as a circus came from the numerous upcoming acts that were offered as entertainment along Ocean Front Walk. There were comedy acts, musicians, jugglers, fireblowers, and an occasional guru. Ex-Swami X, a bearded modern day Lenny Bruce, dressed in sunglasses and a straw hat, stood on a park bench and rapped about the state of the union, drugs and oral sex. He read pages of one-liners, horoscope jokes and pearls of wisdom to more than a hundred people at a time who gathered around him. His speech was punctuated by obscenities, and though certainly was not for young ears, it was entertaining if not enlightening.

Harry Parry, a white turbaned black mystic with steel blue eyes, wearing Indian shirts, hockey shin-pads and roller skates could be seen cruising along the board-walk. He played an electric guitar plugged into a battery powered amplifier that he carried in his backpack. He sang staccato lyrics about 'messages from another world' and 'the propagation of the human species'. Harry preached his message then holding out his cupped hand begged for donations.

The majority of the entertainers in those years were either musicians or jugglers. Jingles and Frank were an unlikely pair, 'the odd couple of music', who played folk and rock & roll music on their guitars. Jingles, the colorful half of the pair, gave tiny bells to his apprecia-tive audience. David and Roselyn were another very popular folk group. She was black and he was white. Their love for wandering the country eventually allowed them time to return to Venice only each spring. Slavin' David and his four man rock & roll style band outlasted them all.

There were very few child entertainers but two thirteen year olds, after failing to make much money as mimes, developed an act called the "Poor Man's Juke Box". They set out an empty refrigerator box on the boardwalk, wrote the name of the available songs next to the coin slots, climbed inside, and waited for customers. One played the kazoo, the other played the side of the box as a drum. The audience's favorite was

'The Yellow Submarine'.

There was a time in late 1977 when city officials tried to stop the street entertainment. The police were told to hassle the street musicians who played "illegally" on public property. Jingles organized the Street Musicians Union to fight the ban, and in 1978 they staged a concert on the grass at the pavilion to publicize their right to play on public property and solicit donations. Twelve musical groups played to an enthusiastic crowd of 5000.

The years 1979-1981 marked the high point in Venice street art. Terry Schoonhoven, the last member of the L.A. Fine Arts Squad, painted his mammoth 50 x 100 foot "St Charles Mural" on the side of the hotel. He painted a scene as if the building were a mirror reflecting the Windward street scene. It was a moment frozen in time, a deserted downtown street on a cold wintery morning where mountains clearly showed in the distance. The scene was purposely left empty to be populated by the viewer.

It was the same year that John Wehrle painted his famous Western-version of "The Fall of Icarus" on a wall along Market Street. The cars in the parking lot facing the mural looked like they were an extension of the deserted desert landscape of an outdoor movie theater. The scene showed a cowboy on a pinto and an angel in the back of an old pickup truck watching a movie of an astronaut floating above the earth, while Icarus plunged to the ground nearby.

There were numerous other murals along the ocean front particularly in the picnic area at the Venice Pavilion. Different groups painted the surrounding walls with scenes of Venice's past. Eventually funding for these mural projects dried up, and others who would have liked to contribute saw the graffiti artist's desecration of the existing murals as reason not to waste their talent.

The two block stretch along the boardwalk on either side of Windward became a gourmet's delight as food vending became international in scope. The exotic aroma of culinary dishes from the four corners of the world led tourists by their noses to stands offering Moroccan cuscous, Mexican tacos and churros, Italian sausage, Middle Eastern flafel, and Japanese teryaki chicken. Hot dog, orange juice, pretzel and popcorn vendors sold from pushcarts in the middle of the walk. Naturally they competed with established restaurants who vehemently complained. But it was the few cases of food poisoning that finally shut them all down.

Los Angeles passed a law in 1982 that prohibited vending on public property, and only those who were

protected by first amendment rights or were legitimate artists or entertainers working for donations were allowed to stay. But performers had to be subtle about passing the hat or they risked a heavy fine.

The vendors were doing especially well despite rapidly rising rents along the Ocean Front Walk. The significantly higher rents however did change the overall character of the merchandise. Artists and others who made hand made goods could no longer afford the $600 / month or more that landlords were asking for 10 x 20 foot vendor spaces. An influx of Koreans selling sunglasses, tennis shoes, backpacks, two dollar watches and 4 for $10 T-shirts, became the norm.

Venice had become so popular by 1984 that it inched into the number two tourist attraction in Southern California just behind Disneyland. When 135 nations attended the Games of the Twenty Third Olympiad, it was on the must see list of numerous athletes and international visitors. ABC camera crews featured daily scenes of breakdancers, comedy acts, jugglers, weight-lifters and musicians along the boardwalk, gorgeous bikini clad California girls suntaning on the wide sandy beach, and surfers riding endless waves just offshore. Venice hosted a crowd like no other, an endless parade of travellers who communicated the best they could by sign language or pidgin English. They like the millions who preceeded them, found Venice to be a unique experience, the most alive place in Los Angeles.

Some say that Venice's boardwalk is improving and others believe that it is getting worse. It has become more crowded, noisier and dirtier. The crowds have become more diverse, more ethnic, more cosmopolitan, more third world, less educated, less involved, more apathetic. Perhaps people are only responding to a sensory overload, or they don't care. Certainly its exaggerated by the mentality of the local teens and young adults whose lifestyle is hang out at the beach and party. They drop out of school, get a part time job (if any) and lead a vagabond life down by the beach. The police stop the beer drinking, but they are powerless to stop the drug dealing. The local gangs feel Venice is their beach and they can trash it if they choose. It looks like a slum, graffiti everywhere, homeless people bumming quarters and the crazies making a nuisance of themselves, but fortunately the tens of thousands of visitors and hundreds of vendors mask it and transform it into a magical carnival, a place to people watch.

Certainly the acts have become better, slick and polished. Bob Gruenberg, the Chainsaw Juggler, on breaks between television specials, still juggles a

(opposite page clockwise from top) A street performer blows fire along Ocean Front Walk; 1983. Venice skaters at Pavilion slalom course; 1979. David and Roselyn, street musicians; 1981. View along Ocean Front Walk looking north from Windward Avenue; 1981.

Robert Gruenberg, 'Venice Chainsaw Juggler' juggles a running chainsaw, tennis ball, and apple; 1985. (above)
'Muscle Beach, an outdoor weightlifting area along Ocean Front Walk; 1983. (top right)
Fall of Icarus mural at Market Street and Speedway; 1979.

running chainsaw. But his act has evolved into a comedy routine. He likes the spirited exchange of insulting the crowd, with some of the language not suitable for prime time.

Perry Hernandez 'Prime Minster of Limbo' gets the crowd chanting "Ooga, Ooga, Yia, Yia." He grinds his bare feet into a pile of broken glass then challenges three bystanders to "Press my ass to the glass!". He lays down on freshly broken liquor bottles while three people stand on his chest and stomach. Afterwards the crowd is amazed that there isn't a scratch on his back.

There are others like Uncle Ray, who can play two trumpets and a foot drum all at once. One black comedian from New York City, for a finale, places a child on a chair, lifts it high in the air by one leg and balances it on his chin. If that doesn't impress the crowd nothing will.

Then there are colorful people who seem like they have been there forever. Everyone has seen Brooks, a short mustached man, who demonstrates his glass pipes by smoking parsley. "Imagine that this is the last of some really sensational tobacco that you have hocked your car and paid through the teeth to get", he teases. The audience draws closer. "Once you light up nothing falls out. Amaze your friends! Always a hit on the house."

It is easy to spot Skateboard Mama, the 62 year old German skateboarding grandmother who slaloms through the cones. She wears a bright pink or yellow sweatshirt emblazoned with her nickname. And there is Jeff the Postcard Man who sells his photographic postcards from a tricycle on the boardwalk, and defies the Chamber of Commerce by selling his hand-drawn cartoon map that they banned. They are all rugged individuals who march to a different drummer.

Everyone who comes to Venice finds it a very special place. They come to see its carnival festive atmosphere, not realizing they will become part of it. Venice gives people a sense of freedom like no where else. It is a place where they can open up and be themselves. That is the real magic of Venice.

Jeffrey Stanton, author of this book, sells his own photographic postcards on Ocean Front Walk near Windward mainly on weekends. He is author of a previous Venice history book 'Venice of America 1905-1930', a photo essay called 'Summer is Forever' about the Southern California beach towns, and eleven computer books including two textbooks on arcade game design. He has two engineering degrees from Rensselaer Polytechnic Institute.